*P*ICK *T*HE *R*IGHT *W*INE

*The Only Comprehensive
and Foolproof Guide to Matching
Specific Foods with Specific Wines*

Daniel McCarthy

DOUBLEDAY
New York   London   Toronto
Sydney   Auckland

PUBLISHED BY DOUBLEDAY
a division of
Bantam Doubleday Dell Publishing Group, Inc.
666 Fifth Avenue, New York, New York 10103

DOUBLEDAY and the portrayal of an
anchor with a dolphin
are registered trademarks of Doubleday,
a division of Bantam Doubleday
Dell Publishing Group, Inc.

Library of Congress
Cataloging-in-Publication Data
McCarthy, Daniel, 1951–
Pick the right wine : the only comprehensive and
foolproof guide to matching specific foods with
specific wines / Daniel McCarthy. — 1st ed.
p.   cm.
1. Food. 2. Wine and wine making.   I. Title.
TX353.M393   1991
641.2'2—dc20   91-2636
CIP
ISBN 0-385-41986-4

BOOK DESIGN BY CAROL MALCOLM

*T*O JILL,

*my wife
and the cook who made this
book possible.*

ACKNOWLEDGMENTS:

I wish to thank all of the patrons of Mc-Carthy & Schiering Wine Merchants, Inc., who over the years have provided the resource for this book. I wish to thank Jay T. Schiering, my partner and friend, who edited the selections, consulted with me over the preparations, and kept the wine shops running while I researched and wrote. Also, Providence Cicero whose belief in the need for this book found it a home, and Judy Kern, my editor at Doubleday, whose encouragement, support, and sense of humor added color to this book. In addition, thanks to the staff of the wine shops, the many wholesalers, importers, brokers, and winery representatives who provided information and samples, and to the winemakers on all continents who produce the wines this book recommends.

CONTENTS

P A S T A   D I S H E S

BUYING AND STORING WINE, AND PARTY PLANNING

INTRODUCTION

Among the hundreds of wine books available, there wasn't a one that went into any detail in recommending specific wines to go with specific food dishes—what a wine merchant does for a living. Most wine books are marvelous achievements, dwelling at length on the origins, producers, laws, and aging potential of wines from various areas. But these books are not quick-reference guides for a wine-shopper who usually wishes to spend fifteen minutes or less in a store, selecting the most appropriate wine for a particular meal.

Wine-buying shouldn't require a degree in wine history any more than preparing a good meal requires a degree in the culinary arts. Where a wine is from, when and how it was made, are very different concerns from how it tastes and which types of food it complements.

This book is a collection of food and wine pairings, organized in an easy-to-use format for consumers who are planning a meal. It would be impossible to list every dish or preparation of food. So, too, it would be impossible to match the wines of every winery with specific meals. Thus, this book is subjective in its nature. Yet, I hope and trust that it will be a starting point for people wishing to

explore what is truly the bounty of the earth . . . fine wine with great food.

Bon appétit.

Daniel McCarthy

HOW TO USE THIS BOOK

The wine business can appear exceptionally confusing to a beginning winebuyer. There are many methods of labeling and thousands of different labels and styles of wine. A first visit to a wine shop or the wine section of a liquor or grocery store can be truly mystifying. How does one know what to try? Consumers seem to be embarrassed about asking "stupid" questions. But any wine merchant worthy of the title understands that there are no stupid questions about wine and attempts to elicit questions in order to assist clients.

The publications covering wine are very useful to knowledgeable buyers, but they can scare off beginners by making them wonder if they're doing the right thing. Newcomers to wine often ask how they are supposed to know if what they like is right? Craig Claiborne, in *The New York Times Cookbook,* writes: "For some obscure reason, some authorities seem bent on making the drinking of wine a ritual more complicated than chess. They have succeeded in inhibiting a large section of the public and depriving them of one of the greatest pleasures known to man." I hope this book will enable its readers to find more easily a path to pleasure by making it simple to choose an appropriate wine for a specific meal.

Over the past ten years of serving customers in my wine shops, one question has been asked time after time, "What do I serve with . . . ?" This book attempts to answer that question by looking at food and wine pairings in a subjective manner and offering both general and specific wine recommendations that complement a wide variety of foods.

However, there are many factors to be considered in following these recommendations. First, this book is a listing of suggestions, but there are many other wines made by many producers that might also match the various dishes. To mention them all is not feasible and would make the book too long to be useful as a quick-reference guide. Second, readers should not expect that all of these wines will be readily available in every market. The selections are meant to be a guide. If you don't find a specific wine, ask your local wine merchant for one in the style similar to those listed. He or she should be able to make an appropriate substitution. Third, the price of wine varies widely around the country. The listed price ranges are stated only to give the reader an idea of what the type of wine may cost. Lastly, with each new vintage, there is a completely new set of wines to review. Thus, though at the time of publication the preferred vintages were current, the information in this book has a time value.

HOW TO READ AN ENTRY

Example:

California Cabernet Sauvignon Producers
Caymus Vineyards *Napa Valley*†
Look for Special Selection
Price Range $15–40
Preferred Vintages '85, '86 ('87 to cellar)

Each recommendation has two parts, the general and the specific wine recommendation:

GENERAL WINE RECOMMENDATION

California Cabernet Sauvignon Producers

• The general wine recommendation is listed first and includes the country (or state) of origin and the grape variety or growing region. Most American wines are classified by their grape variety, e.g., California Cabernet Sauvignon or Washington Chardonnay. European wines usually are classified by their area of origin, e.g., Italian Chianti or French Bordeaux.

• It is important to note that the general wine recommendation is the key information. Most wines of this type will match the specific food preparation. The specific recommendations are excellent choices, but if they are not available, use the general wine recommendation to find other wines that complement the food.

SPECIFIC WINE RECOMMENDATION

Caymus Vineyards *Napa Valley*†
Look for Special Selection

• The specific wine recommendation (Caymus Vineyards) is the brand name of the producer whose wine is being recommended. (*The producer sometimes uses a proprietary name for the wine. This is listed in single quotes after the producer's name.*)

• The appellation (*Napa Valley*) is listed following the brand name. The appellation is the legal designation for the region where the grapes were grown. It may be a valley, river, or county name, a state, commune or parish, or a district. This information is included only when pertinent.

• The symbol "†" follows recommendations of specific wines that may be hard to find but are well worth seeking out.

• If there is a specific vineyard, or a reserve or special bottling to look for, this will be listed in smaller type below the specific wine recommendation. (In this case "Look for Special Selection").

Following the specific wine recommendations for each entry are two useful pieces of information, price range and preferred vintages:

Price Range $15–40

• Wine prices vary substantially across the country. The price range is included to give the user an idea of approximately how much the wine should cost. The standard bottlings are likely to be priced at the lower end of the price range, and reserve or special bottlings are likely to be at the higher end.

Preferred Vintages '85, '86 ('87 to cellar)

• The preferred vintages listed reflect both the best quality vintages for the wine type and those years most likely to be available in stores. My first choice is underlined. (*Note: Preferred vintages are omitted where not applicable or where available vintages vary between producers.*)

Following the specific wine recommendations are alternative suggestions for modestly priced or widely distributed wines:

Value Recommendation
• Wherever possible, I have tried to match the value of the wine to the type of meal being prepared. In some cases this may result in a more expensive wine than desired. When the price of the general wine recommendations exceeds $12 per bottle, I have included a value recommendation for a wine with a price of less than $12 per bottle. The value recommendation is particularly useful for family gatherings or larger groups.

Easy-to-Find or Alternative Selection
• Some of the recommended wines may not be readily available in all wine shops, or liquor or grocery store wine sections. At the end of each entry there is an easy-to-find or alternative selection, which is a wine from a nationally distributed brand that goes nicely with

the dish. Because of the limited number of wines that have broad market distribution, some repetition of these recommendations is unavoidable.

Appetizers

Many of the dishes listed in this book as main courses can also be served as appetizers. But there are a few common appetizers that usually aren't served as main courses.

CAVIAR

The slightly salty flavor and very delicate texture of good caviar calls for sparkling wine. Very few still wines are as flavorful yet delicate as French Champagne. Listed are the nonvintage brut wines of each firm. The Tête de Cuvée wines are the premium blends from particular French Champagne houses. Good quality California and Italian sparkling wines are also a nice match for caviar.

French Champagne Producers

Veuve Clicquot-Ponsardin Brut *Reims*
Tête de Cuvée: La Grande Dame
Louis Roederer Brut Premier *Reims*
Tête de Cuvée: Cristal
Taittinger Brut La Française *Reims*
Tête de Cuvée: Comtes de Champagne
Bollinger Special Cuvée *Aÿ*
Tête de Cuvée: Vieilles Vignes Françaises
Gosset Grande Réserve Brut *Aÿ†*
Tête de Cuvée: Grand Millésime

Moët & Chandon Brut Imperial *Épernay*
Tête de Cuvée: Dom Pérignon
Perrier-Jouët Grand Brut *Épernay*
Tête de Cuvée: Fleur de Champagne
Price Range $25–125
Preferred Vintages (nonvintage)
'79 '82 '83 '85 for Têtes de Cuvée

California Sparkling Wine Producers

Roederer Estate Brut *Anderson Valley*†
Van der Kamp Brut *Sonoma Valley*†
Domaine Carneros Brut *Napa Valley*
Maison Deutz Brut *Santa Barbara*
Michel Tribaut Brut *Monterey*†
Schramsberg Blanc de Blancs *Napa Valley*
Price Range $13–25

Italian Sparkling Wine Producers

Bruno Giacosa Extra Brut *Piedmont*
Berlucchi Cuvée Imperiale Brut *Lombardy*
Carpené Malvolti Brut *Veneto*
Venegazzù Brut *Veneto*
Bortolomiol Brut *Valdobbiadene*†
Price Range $8–30

Value Recommendations

Domaine Ste. Michelle Champagne Brut
   Washington
Freixenet Cordon Negro *Spain*
Price Range $7–12

Easy-to-Find or Alternative Selections
Domaine Chandon Brut *Napa Valley*
Price Range $9–15

Mumm Cordon Rouge *Reims*
Price Range $28–35

CHEESES

The range of cheeses is vast and the
different textures and flavors seem

endless. But in general, most cheeses go well with full-bodied whites and medium-bodied reds. Each wine should have firm acidity to cleanse the palate. The marriage of wine and cheese has been well documented in cookbooks, and there is no end to the potential wine and cheese combinations. A few matches are especially tasty. For double cream and triple cream cheeses, California Chardonnay and Italian Pinot Grigio are good choices. With cheddars and hard cheeses, Italian Chianti, Classico is a nice match.

California Chardonnay Producers

Newton Vineyards *Napa Valley*
Château St. Jean *Sonoma*
Matanzas Creek *Sonoma*
De Loach Vineyards *Sonoma*
Innisfree *Napa Valley*
Morgan Winery *Monterey*
Price Range $12–18
Preferred Vintages '88, '89, '90

Italian Pinot Grigio Producers

Gianni Vescovo
Borgo Conventi†
Livio Felluga
Bollini
Price Range $10–17
Preferred Vintages '89, '90

Italian Chianti Classico Producers

Fattoria di Felsina
Fontodi

Frescobaldi
Antinori
Rocca delle Macie
Monsanto
Price Range $8–15
Preferred Vintages '87, '88, '89

Easy to Find or Alternative Selections

Robert Mondavi Winery Chardonnay
  'Woodbridge' *California*
Price Range $7–10
Preferred Vintages '89, '90
Santa Margherita Pinot Grigio
Price Range $14–17
Preferred Vintages '89, '90

OLIVES

With green olives, Spanish Fino and
Manzanilla sherries are a perfect
complement. For Niçoise and black
olives, try a bottle of French Corbières
Blanc or Cassis Blanc.

**Spanish Fino and Manzanilla Sherry
Producers**

Valdespiño Fino 'Ynocente'
Hidalgo Manzanilla 'La Gitana'
Gonzalez Byass
Osborne 'Fino Quinta'
Emilio Lustau
Look for Almacenista Reserva
Pedro Domecq 'La Ina'
Price Range $7–15

**French Corbières Blanc and Cassis Blanc
Producers**

Mont Tauch†
Rogue Sestière†

Domaine de Fontsainte 'Gris de Gris'†
Clos Ste. Magdelaine Cassis Blanc†
Price Range $7–14
Preferred Vintages '88, '89

Easy-to-Find or Alternative Selections
Gonzalez Byass 'Tio Pepe' Fino Sherry
Price Range $8–12

La Vieille Ferme Côtes du Lubéron Blanc
Price Range $5–8
Preferred Vintages '88, '89, '90

PÂTÉ

The rich flavor and texture of pâté require a white or red wine with firm acidity. I suggest a French Bourgogne Blanc or Bourgogne Rouge as an excellent match. But many other wines are also nice alternatives. Look to the theme of the main course for the country or style of the wine. In France, it is popular to serve a glass of young Sauternes with pâté de fois gras.

French Bourgogne Blanc Producers

Louis Jadot
Hervé Roumier†
Coche-Dury†
Chartron & Trébuchet
Bouchard Père & Fils
Price Range $10–18
Preferred Vintages '88, '89

French Bourgogne Rouge Producers

Joseph Faiveley
Philippe Rossignol†

Bernard Serveau†
Joseph Drouhin 'Laforet'
Mongeard-Mugneret†
Price Range $10–18
Preferred Vintages '88, '89

French Sauternes Producers

Château Rieussec *Sauternes*
Château Filhot *Sauternes*
Château Nairac *Sauternes*†
Château Rabaud-Promis *Sauternes*†
Château Les Justices *Sauternes*
Château de Malle *Sauternes*
Price Range $14–30 (in 375 ml bottles)
Preferred Vintages '83, '86, '88, ('89 to cellar)

Easy-to-Find or Alternative Selections

Joseph Drouhin Bourgogne Blanc 'Laforet'
Price Range $9–12
Preferred Vintages '89, '90
Robert Mondavi Winery Pinot Noir *Napa Valley*
Price Range $14–18
Preferred Vintages '88, '89

QUICHE

There are many ways to prepare quiche, each with different ingredients to consider, but the basis is always cream and eggs. White wines with good acidity such as Alsatian Riesling and Oregon Pinot Gris are excellent. California Sauvignon Blanc is also pleasing with quiche.

Alsatian Riesling Producers

Domaine Weinbach†
F. E. Trimbach
Zind-Humbrecht
Look for Réserve†
Hugel
Price Range $9–20
Preferred Vintages '88, '89
(Additionally, the firm of Láugel makes Crémant d'Alsace sparkling wine, which is excellent with quiche.)

Oregon Pinot Gris Producers

Adelsheim Vineyard *Oregon*†
The Eyrie Vineyards *Willamette Valley*
Ponzi Vineyards *Oregon*†
Rex Hill Vineyards *Oregon*†
Price Range $9–14
Preferred Vintages '89, '90

California Sauvignon Blanc Producers

Babcock Vineyards *Santa Ynez Valley*
Look for Eleven Oaks†
Duckhorn Vineyards *Napa Valley*†
Silverado Vineyards *Napa Valley*
Kenwood Vineyards *Sonoma County*
Robert Pepi *Napa Valley*
Benziger *Sonoma*
Price Range $8–15
Preferred Vintages '89, '90

Easy-to-Find or Alternative Selections

Beringer Vineyards Sauvignon Blanc *Napa Valley*
Price Range $7–10
Preferred Vintages '89, '90

Hogue Cellars Fumé Blanc *Washington State*
Price Range $7–10
Preferred Vintages '89, '90

SOUPS

The range of soups includes everything from consommé to gazpacho. Look to the specific ingredients as well as the theme of the entire meal to select the appropriate wine.

CONSOMMÉ

The beef flavor of consommé is nicely matched by a white Bordeaux as well as a soft Pinot Noir such as a French Bourgogne Rouge. Sancerre Rouge is a beautiful combination, but it can be difficult to find.

French White Bordeaux Producers

Château de Launay *Entre-Deux-Mers*
Château Bonnet *Entre-Deux-Mers*
Domaine Challon *Bordeaux*
Château La Louvière Blanc *Pessac Léognan*
Château Rahoul *Graves*†
Price Range $7–18
Preferred Vintages '88, '89, '90

French Bourgogne Rouge Producers

Joseph Drouhin 'Laforet'
Bernard Serveau†
Louis Jadot
Bouchard Père & Fils
Price Range $9–18
Preferred Vintages '88, '89

French Sancerre Rouge Producers

Henri Bourgeois†
Hippolyte Reverdy†
Jean-Max Roger†
Price Range $12–18
Preferred Vintages '87, '88, '89

Easy-to-Find or Alternative Selections

La Vieille Ferme Côtes du Ventoux Rouge
Price Range $5–8
Preferred Vintages '88, '89, '90

Maître d'Estournel *Bordeaux*
Price Range $7–10
Preferred Vintages '88, '89, '90

CREAMY
VEGETABLE SOUP

To match the flavor of creamy
vegetable soup, buttery white wines
such as California Chardonnay or
Australian Chardonnay are excellent.

California Chardonnay Producers

Zaca Mesa *Santa Barbara County*
Raymond *Napa Valley*
Babcock Vineyards *Santa Ynez Valley*
St. Gregory *Mendocino*†
La Crema *California*
Franciscan Vineyards *Napa Valley*
Price Range $9–16
Preferred Vintages '88, '89, '90

Australian Chardonnay Producers

Rothbury Estate *Hunter Valley*
Wyndham Estate *Southeastern Australia*

Seppelt *South Australia*
Montrose *Mudgee*†
Price Range $7–15
Preferred Vintages '87, '89, '90

Easy-to-Find or Alternative Selections

Fetzer Vineyards Chardonnay 'Barrel Select'
    Mendocino
Price Range $9–12
Preferred Vintages '89, '90

Lindeman's Chardonnay 'Bin 65'
    Southeastern Australia
Price Range $6–9
Preferred Vintage '90

GAZPACHO

The liquid salad of Spain, gazpacho has
a spicy tomato, cucumber, and onion
flavor accented with garlic, and it
deserves a bottle of either white or red
wine from Spain.

Spanish White Wine Producers

Torres *Penedés*
Look for Gran Viña Sol
Montecillo *Rioja*
Marqués de Cáceres *Rioja*
Labastida *Rioja*
Martinsancho Verdejo *Rueda*†
Price Range $7–15
Preferred Vintages '88, '89, '90

Spanish Red Rioja Producers

Berberana
Bodegas Olarra
La Rioja Alta

Marqués de Riscal
Marqués de Cáceres
Bodegas Bretón 'Loriñón'†
Price Range $8–15
Preferred Vintages '85, '87, '88 *('89 to cellar)*

Spanish Ribera del Duero Producers

Tinto Pesquera†
Balbás†
Viña Pedrosa†
Price Range $7–18
Preferred Vintages '85, '86, '88 *('89 to cellar)*

Easy-to-Find or Alternative Selections

Torres Viña Sol *Penedés*
Torres Sangre de Toro *Penedés*
Price Range $5–8
Preferred Vintages '88, '89, '90

FRENCH ONION SOUP

French onion soup is rich, sweet, and topped with melted cheese. A bottle of French Bourgogne Blanc is just about the perfect combination, but the cherry-like flavor of French Bourgogne Rouge and Oregon Pinot Noir is also a fine match.

French Bourgogne Blanc Producers

Louis Jadot
Michel Juillot†
Chartron & Trébuchet

Olivier Leflaive†
Labouré-Roi
Price Range $10–18
Preferred Vintages '88, '89

French Bourgogne Rouge Producers

Joseph Drouhin 'Laforet'
Robert Chevillon†
Joseph Faiveley
Louis Latour
Louis Jadot
Price Range $9–18
Preferred Vintages '88, '89

Oregon Pinot Noir Producers

Sokol Blosser Winery *'Redland'*†
Knudsen Erath Winery *Oregon*
Look for Vintage Select
Amity Vineyards *Oregon*†
Adelsheim Vineyard *Willamette Valley*†
Bethel Heights Vineyard *Willamette Valley*†
Price Range $10–18
Preferred Vintages '88, '89

Easy-to-Find or Alternative Selections

Joseph Drouhin Bourgogne Blanc 'Laforet'
Price Range $9–12
Preferred Vintages '89, '90

J. Pedroncelli Pinot Noir *Sonoma County*
Price Range $9–12
Preferred Vintages '87, '88

LENTIL OR BEAN SOUP

Rich and filling, lentil or bean soup requires a crisp white to cleanse the palate. Try an Alsatian Riesling or Pinot Blanc, or a California Semillon.

Alsatian Riesling Producers

Gustave Lorentz
F. E. Trimbach
Zind-Humbrecht
Look for Réserve†
Hugel
Price Range $9–20
Preferred Vintages '88, '89

Alsatian Pinot Blanc Producers

Gustave Lorentz
Look for Réserve
F. E. Trimbach
Zind-Humbrecht
Hugel
Price Range $8–18
Preferred Vintages '88, '89

California Semillon Producers

Alderbrook Winery *Dry Creek Valley*
Duckhorn Vineyards 'Decoy' *Napa Valley*†
Benziger *Sonoma*
Price Range $7–12
Preferred Vintages '88, '89, '90

Easy-to-Find or Alternative Selections

Hogue Cellars Dry Riesling *Washington State*
Chateau Ste. Michelle Semillon Blanc
   Columbia Valley
Price Range $5–8
Preferred Vintages '89, '90

SEAFOOD BISQUE

The spices and the different flavors of the seafood in a bisque call for a Sauvignon Blanc. Try a white Bordeaux or a California Sauvignon Blanc with crisp acidity. Washington Sauvignon Blanc also goes well with seafood bisque.

French White Bordeaux Producers

Château de Launay *Entre-Deux-Mers*
Château Bonnet *Entre-Deux-Mers*
Chevalier de Védrines *Bordeaux*
Château La Louvière Blanc *Pessac Léognan*
Domaine la Grave *Graves*†
Price Range $7–18
Preferred Vintages '88, '89, '90

California Sauvignon Blanc Producers

Silverado Vineyards *Napa Valley*
Kenwood Vineyards *Sonoma County*
Clos Pegase *Napa Valley*
Iron Horse Ranch & Vineyards *Sonoma*
Chimney Rock *Napa Valley*†
Price Range $7–12
Preferred Vintages '89, '90

Washington Sauvignon Blanc Producers

Arbor Crest *Columbia Valley*†
Hogue Cellars *Washington State*
Paul Thomas *Washington*†
Chinook *Yakima Valley*†
Cavatappi Winery *Washington*†
Price Range $7–12
Preferred Vintages '89, '90

Beringer Vineyards Sauvignon Blanc
  California
Price Range $7–10
Preferred Vintages '89, '90

Maître d'Estournel *Bordeaux*
Price Range $7–10
Preferred Vintages '88, '89, '90

TOMATO SOUP OR MINESTRONE

Tomato-based soups, when served
warm, have a flavor that goes well with
Italian Orvieto Classico or Verdicchio.
The only rule is to avoid a wine with too
much body.

Italian Orvieto Classico Producers

Barbi
Barberani
Bigi†
Decugnano dei Barbi†
Antinori
Ruffino
Price Range $7–12
Preferred Vintages '89, '90

Italian Verdicchio Producers

Colonnara 'Cuprese'
Garafoli†
Look for Macrina
Fazi-Battaglia
Umani Ronchi
Look for Casal di Sera
Price Range $7–14
Preferred Vintages (*youngest available*)

TURKEY SOUP

Filled with rice or noodles and vegetables, turkey soup is great to have with a bottle of American dry Riesling or Chenin Blanc. Beaujolais Nouveau also makes a pleasant accompaniment.

American Dry Riesling Producers

Trefethen Vineyards *Napa Valley*
Amity Vineyards 'Dry' *Oregon*†
Ste. Chapelle 'Dry' *Idaho*†
Price Range $5–10
Preferred Vintages '88, '89, '90

American Dry Chenin Blanc Producers

Snoqualmie Winery *Washington*
Villa Mt. Eden Winery *Napa Valley*
Folie-à-Deux *Napa Valley*†
Girard Winery *Napa Valley*
Seghesio *Russian River Valley*
Price Range $7–10
Preferred Vintages '89, '90

French Beaujolais Nouveau Producers

Georges Duboeuf
Sylvain Fessy†
Mommessin
Bouchard Père & Fils
Price Range $9–14
Preferred Vintages (only the current release)
(American producers of Gamay are also worth mentioning. In California, Robert Pepi, Charles Shaw, and Preston Vineyards & Winery all make fruity and flavorful Gamay. Amity Vineyards in Oregon produces an excellent Gamay Noir.)

Chateau Ste. Michelle Dry Riesling *Columbia
Valley*
Hogue Cellars Dry Riesling Reserve
Washington
Price Range $4–7
Preferred Vintages '89, '90

VICHYSSOISE

Cream, leeks, and potatoes give
vichyssoise a unique flavor. Since it is
usually served chilled, it will stand up to
the complex flavor of Spanish
Manzanilla sherry. An Alsatian Pinot
Blanc or a dry white Bordeaux also go
well with this soup.

Spanish Manzanilla Sherry Producers

Hidalgo 'La Gitana'
Osborne
Barbadillo†
Emilio Lustau
Look for Almacenista Reserva
Price Range $7–15

Alsatian Pinot Blanc Producers

Gustave Lorentz
Zind-Humbrecht
Hugel
Price Range $12–20
Preferred Vintages '88, '89

French White Bordeaux Producers

Château Bonnet *Entre-Deux-Mers*
Château de Launay *Entre-Deux-Mers*

Château Respide-Médeville *Graves*
Château Ferrande *Castres*
Domaine Challon *Bordeaux*
Price Range $7–13
Preferred Vintages *'88, '89, '90*

Easy-to-Find or Alternative Selection

F. E. Trimbach Pinot Blanc
Price Range $9–12
Preferred Vintages *'88, '89*

BEEF

As a simple rule, stick with red wines to match the flavor and texture of beef. The age of the wine also becomes an important consideration. Older, softer reds more evenly match the taste of well-aged beef. Barrel-aged reds are softer and have depth and complexity when young.

BEEF BOURGUIGNON

This country dish owes its name to the wine region of Burgundy where it was popularized. The best match for the slightly sweet and hearty flavor of this stew is a bottle of Bourgogne Rouge or a Bourgogne Passetoutgrains. Bourgogne Passetoutgrains is hard to find, but an Oregon Pinot Noir is a good substitute.

French Bourgogne Rouge Producers

Joseph Drouhin 'Laforet'
Robert Chevillon†
Joseph Faiveley
Remoissenet 'Renommée'†
Louis Jadot
Price Range $9–18
Preferred Vintages '88, '89

French Bourgogne Passetoutgrains Producers

Louis Valpato†
Jean Tardy†
Louis Jadot
Price Range $8–12
Preferred Vintages '88, '89

Oregon Pinot Noir Producers

Sokol Blosser Winery 'Redland'†
Knudsen Erath Winery *Oregon*
Look for vintage select.
Panther Creek Cellars *Willamette Valley*†
Amity Vineyards *Oregon*†
Chateau Benoit *Oregon*†
Adelsheim Vineyard *Willamette Valley*†
Bethel Heights Vineyard *Willamette Valley*†
Price Range $10–18
Preferred Vintages '88, '89

Easy-to-Find or Alternative Selections

La Vieille Ferme Côtes du Ventoux Rouge
Price Range $5–8
Preferred Vintages '88, '89 '90
J. Pedroncelli Pinot Noir *Sonoma County*
Price Range $9–12
Preferred Vintages '87, '88

BEEF STROGANOFF

The mushrooms and sour cream in this dish are the tastes to match. A good bottle of Côtes-du-Rhône Rouge or Côtes du Ventoux from the Rhône Valley is well suited to this preparation. Also, a lighter California Zinfandel tastes fine with beef stroganoff.

French Côtes-du-Rhône Rouge Producers

E. Guigal
J. Vidal-Fleury
Château du Trignon
Kermit Lynch Selection
Paul Jaboulet-Aîné 'Parallèle 45'
Price Range $7–12
Preferred Vintages '88, '89 '90

French Côtes du Ventoux Producers

La Vieille Ferme
Paul Jaboulet-Aîné
Price Range $5–10
Preferred Vintages '88, '89, '90

California Zinfandel Producers

Quivira *Sonoma County*†
Cuvaison *Napa Valley*†
Burgess Cellars *Napa Valley*
Rafanelli Winery *Sonoma*†
Ravenswood 'Vintner's Blend' *Sonoma*
Price Range $7–13
Preferred Vintages '87, '88, '89

Easy-to-Find or Alternative Selection

Round Hill Vineyards Zinfandel *California*
Price Range $6–9
Preferred Vintages '88, '89

CORNED BEEF

This classic New England boiled dinner
has a wide variety of flavors to match,
and corned beef has a rich, almost oily
texture. My preference is a young
Beaujolais-Villages but a Long Island
Merlot also complements corned beef.

French Beaujolais-Villages Producers

Joseph Drouhin
Louis Latour
Louis Jadot
Sylvain Fessy†
Louis Trenel†
Price Range $7–12
Preferred Vintages '88, '89, '90

New York Merlot Producers

Bedell Cellars *Long Island*†
Bidwell Vineyards *Long Island*†
Hargrave Vineyard *Long Island*†
Pindar Vineyards *Long Island*†
Price Range $10–20
Preferred Vintages '88, '89

Easy-to-Find or Alternative Selection

Georges Duboeuf Beaujolais-Villages
Price Range $7–10
Preferred Vintages '89, '90

FILET MIGNON

Filet mignon deserves the finest red
Burgundy one can afford. Sauces vary
from béarnaise to red wine reductions,
but none is too overpowering for a great
Pinot Noir from the Côte d'Or. Claret
lovers would surely argue that a well-
aged bottle of classified growth
Bordeaux is superior, but either one
meets my standards. There are many
price ranges for Burgundy and
Bordeaux, and I have listed the rare and
often expensive wines separately.

French Red Burgundy Producers

GEVREY-CHAMBERTIN
Louis Jadot
Look for Clos des Corvées
Philippe LeClerc†
Look for Combe aux Moines

VOSNE-ROMANÉE
Henri Jayer†
Look for Les Brûlées
René Engel†
Look for Les Brûlées
Jean Gros†
Look for Clos des Réas

NUITS-ST.-GEORGES
Jean Grivot
Look for Les Roncières
Robert Chevillon†
Price Range $30–60
Preferred Vintages '85, '87, '88

Rare French Red Burgundy Producers

LA TÂCHE
Domaine de la Romanée-Conti†

ROMANÉE-CONTI
Domaine de la Romanée-Conti†

CHAMBERTIN
Pierre Bourée†
Domaine Ponsot†
Clos Frantin (Bichot)†
Domaine Armand Rousseau†
Leroy†
Price Range $100–350 +
Preferred Vintages '85, ('88, '89 to cellar)

French Red Bordeaux Producers

Château Pichon-Longueville, Comtesse de
    Lalande *Pauillac*
Château Lynch-Bages *Pauillac*

Château Léoville-Las Cases *St.-Julien*
Château Clerc-Milon *Pauillac*
Château Haut-Bailly *Pessac Léognan*
Château Ducru-Beaucaillou *St.-Julien*
Price Range $25–75
Preferred Vintages '82, '85, ('86, '88, '89 to cellar)

Rare French Red Bordeaux Producers

Château Lafite-Rothschild *Pauillac*†
Château Latour *Pauillac*†
Château Mouton-Rothschild *Pauillac*†
Château Pétrus *Pomerol*†
Château Haut-Brion *Graves*†
Château Margaux *Margaux*†
Price Range $85–250
Preferred Vintages '82, '85, ('86, '88, '89 to cellar)

Value Recommendations

Château La Tour de By *Médoc*
Château Les Garelles 1ᵉʳ *Côtes de Blaye*
Château Bourdillot 1ᵉʳ *Côtes de Blaye*
Château Guiraud-Cheval-Blanc *Côtes de Bourg*
Price Range $7–10
Preferred Vintages '88, '89

J. Pedroncelli Cabernet Sauvignon *Sonoma County*
Monticello Cellars Cabernet Sauvignon 'Jefferson Cuvée' *Napa Valley*
Price Range $9–12
Preferred Vintages '87, '88

Easy-to-Find or Alternative Selections

Beaulieu Vineyards Cabernet Sauvignon 'Rutherford' *Napa Valley*
Robert Mondavi Winery Cabernet Sauvignon *Napa Valley*
Fetzer Vineyards Cabernet Sauvignon 'Barrel Select' *California*
Price Range $12–22
Preferred Vintages '87, '88, '89

NEW YORK STRIP STEAK

The unique flavor of a New York strip steak is wonderful with classic French Bordeaux and great California Cabernet Sauvignon. Also, Washington Cabernet Sauvignon matches its flavor nicely.

French Red Bordeaux Producers

Château Haut-Bailly *Pessac Léognan*
Château de Fieuzal *Pessac Léognan*†
Château La Louvière Rouge *Pessac Léognan*
Château Pape-Clément *Pessac Léognan*
Price Range $25–35
Preferred Vintages '85, '86, '87, ('88, '89 to cellar)

California Cabernet Sauvignon Producers

Laurel Glen *Sonoma Mountain*†
Grgich Hills Cellar *Napa Valley*
Beaulieu Vineyards *Napa Valley*
Look for Private Reserve 'Georges de Latour'
Arrowood Vineyards & Winery *Sonoma County*
Silver Oak Cellars *Alexander Valley*
Clos du Val *Napa Valley*
Price Range $15–30
Preferred Vintages '85, '86, ('87 to cellar)

Washington Cabernet Sauvignon Producers

Woodward Canyon Winery *Washington*†
Chateau Ste. Michelle *Columbia Valley*
Look for Cold Creek Reserve

Quilceda Creek *Washington*†
Seven Hills *Washington*†
Leonetti Cellar *Washington*†
Price Range $12–25
Preferred Vintages '86, '87, ('88, '89 to cellar)

Value Recommendation

Monticello Cellars Cabernet Sauvignon
 'Jefferson Cuvée' *Napa Valley*
Price Range $9–12
Preferred Vintages '87, 88

Easy-to-Find or Alternative Selections

Beringer Vineyards Cabernet Sauvignon
 Knight's Valley
Price Range $10–14
Preferred Vintages '87, 88

Beaulieu Vineyards Cabernet Sauvignon
 'Beautour' *Napa Valley*
Price Range $9–12
Preferred Vintages '87, '88

FLANK STEAK

Once known as a bargain cut, flank
steak has been more recently
"discovered." The rich taste of the juice
and the lean texture of the meat make
Merlot from California or Washington a
perfect match. Another good choice is a
full-flavored Italian Chianti.

California Merlot Producers

Clos du Bois *Sonoma County*
Clos du Val *Napa Valley*
Straus Vineyards *Napa Valley*†
St. Francis *Sonoma County*†

Rombauer Vineyards *Napa Valley*
Markham Winery *Napa Valley*
Price Range $12–20
Preferred Vintages '87, '88, '89

Washington Merlot Producers

Woodward Canyon Winery *Washington*†
Andrew Will *Washington*†
Leonetti Cellar *Washington*†
Gordon Brothers *Washington State*†
Covey Run *Yakima Valley*
Hyatt Vineyards *Yakima Valley*†
Hogue Cellars *Washington State*
Look for Reserve
Price Range $12–25
Preferred Vintages '88, '89

Italian Chianti Producers

Fattoria di Felsina
Look for Riserva
Frescobaldi 'Castello di Nipozzano'
Look for Montesodi
Castello di Volpaia
Fontodi
Ruffino 'Riserva Ducale'
Price Range $8–15
Preferred Vintages '87, '88, '89

Easy-to-Find or Alternative Selections

Columbia Crest Merlot *Columbia Valley*
Price Range $9–12
Preferred Vintages '88, '89
Frescobaldi Chianti Classico
Price Range $5–8
Preferred Vintages '89, '90

HAMBURGERS

Yes, there are great wine recommendations for hamburgers, even those replete with bacon, cheese, onion, tomato, and almost any other condiment save guacamole. A bottle of California Zinfandel is the perfect answer. French Côtes-du-Rhône Rouge is very popular, and a bottle of California red table wine is also a good match.

California Zinfandel Producers

Rafanelli Winery *Sonoma*†
Burgess Cellars *Napa Valley*
Marietta Cellars *Sonoma County*
Karly *Amador County*
DeLoach Vineyards *Sonoma County*
Price Range $7–13
Preferred Vintages '87, '88, '89

French Côtes-du-Rhône Rouge Producers

E. Guigal
J. Vidal-Fleury
Château du Trignon
Kermit Lynch Selection
Price Range $7–12
Preferred Vintages '88, '89, '90

California Red Table Wine Producers

The Monterey Vineyards *California*
R. H. Phillips 'Night Harvest' *California*†
J. Pedroncelli 'Sonoma Red' *Sonoma County*
Price Range 1.5 Liter $8–12
Preferred Vintages (mostly nonvintage)

Easy-to-Find or Alternative Selections
Round Hill Vineyards Red Table *California*
Parducci Red Table *California*
Price Range 1.5 Liter $8–12
Preferred Vintages *(mostly nonvintage)*

PEPPER STEAK

Black pepper, the essential ingredient
in pepper steak, is also the key flavor of
Syrah from the Rhône Valley in France.
Either the spicy, berry-like aroma of
Châteauneuf-du-Pape or the deep, heady
bouquet of Côte-Rôtie or Hermitage is
perfect with this dish. A bottle of
California's better Petite Sirah or Syrah
is also a flavorful accompaniment.

French Red Rhône Valley Producers

CHÂTEAUNEUF-DU-PAPE
Domaine du Vieux Télégraphe
Château de Beaucastel

CÔTE-RÔTIE
René Rostaing†
E. Guigal
A. Dervieux–Thaize†
Look for La Viaillère
Robert Jasmin†

HERMITAGE
Paul Jaboulet-Aîné 'La Chapelle'
J.L. Chave†
Domaine Sorrel†
Look for Le Gréal
Price Range $15–50
Preferred Vintages '85, '86, '88 *('89 to cellar)*

California Petite Sirah / Syrah Producers

Guenoc Winery *Lake County*
McDowell Valley Vineyards *Mendocino*
Ridge Vineyards *'York Creek'*
Nevada County Wine Guild *Sierra Foothills†*
Trentadue *Mendocino*
Joseph Phelps Vineyards *Napa Valley*
Stag's Leap Winery *Napa Valley*
Price Range $8–18
Preferred Vintages '85, '87, '88
(Edmunds St. John in Berkeley, produces a nonvintage American red table wine called 'Les Côtes Sauvage' from a blend of California Syrah and Washington Grenache. Bonny Doon Vineyard in Santa Cruz produces a wine called 'Old Telegram' made from Mourvèdre grapes, and a wine called 'Le Cigare Volant,' which is a blend of Mourvèdre, Grenache, and Syrah. Both are highly recommended. Cline Cellars in Contra Costa County produces an excellent Mourvèdre. *Look for the '88 and '89 vintages.*)

Easy-to-Find or Alternative Selection
E. Guigal Côtes-du-Rhône Rouge
Price Range $10–13
Preferred Vintages '88, '89

PORTERHOUSE STEAK

The meaty taste of properly cooked porterhouse steak calls for a three- to five-year-old St.-Emilion or a bottle of California Cabernet Sauvignon from a producer of big, flavory wine. Washington Cabernet Sauvignon is also very good with porterhouse steak.

French St.-Emilion Producers

Château L'Angelus *St.-Emilion*
Château Canon *St.-Emilion*
Château Figeac *St.-Emilion*
Château Le Tertre-Roteboeuf *St.-Emilion*
Château L'Arrosée *St.-Emilion*
Château La Dominique *St.-Emilion*
Château Clos des Jacobins *St.-Emilion*
Price Range $25–45
Preferred Vintages '85, *'86,* '87 ('88, '89 to
  cellar)

California Cabernet Sauvignon Producers

Newton Vineyards *Napa Valley*
St. Clement Vineyard *Napa Valley*
Steltzner Vineyards *Napa Valley*
Chappellet Vineyard *Napa Valley*
Pine Ridge Winery *Napa Valley*
Chateau Montelena *Napa Valley*
Price Range $15–30
Preferred Vintages '85, '86, '87

Rare California Cabernet Sauvignon Producers

Diamond Creek Vineyards *Napa Valley*†
Look for Red Rock Terrace, Volcanic Hill, Gravelly
Meadow
Beringer Vineyards *Napa Valley*†
Look for Private Reserve
Spottswoode Vineyard & Winery *Napa Valley*†
Caymus Vineyards *Napa Valley*†
Look for Special Selection
Heitz Cellars *Napa Valley*†
Look for Martha's Vineyard
Dunn Vineyards *Napa Valley*†
Look for Howell Mountain
Stag's Leap Wine Cellars *Napa Valley*†
Look for Cask 23

Forman Vineyard *Napa Valley*†
Groth Vineyards *Napa Valley*†
Look for Reserve
Joseph Phelps Vineyards *Napa Valley*
Look for Bacchus Vineyard†
Price Range $35–100 +
Preferred Vintages '85, '86 ('87 to cellar)
(Additionally, the new blends of Cabernet
Sauvignon, Merlot, Cabernet Franc, Petite Verdot,
and other varieties styled in a similar fashion to
French Médoc wines called 'Meritage' can be
enjoyed with porterhouse steak. There are many
now in production. Among them, Opus One,
Dominus, Inglenook 'Reunion,' Floras Springs
'Trilogy,' Carmenet Red, Lyeth Red, Sterling
Vineyards Reserve Red, Nelson Estate Cabernet
Franc, Dry Creek 'Meritage,' Franciscan
'Meritage,' and Optima stand out. *Look for the
'87 vintage.*)

Washington Cabernet Sauvignon Producers

Woodward Canyon Winery *Washington*†
Chateau Ste. Michelle *Columbia Valley*
Look for Cold Creek Reserve
Quilceda Creek *Washington*†
Seven Hills *Washington*†
Leonetti Cellar *Washington*†
Look for Reserve
Hogue Cellars *Washington State*
Look for Reserve
Price Range $12–25
Preferred Vintages '86, '87 ('88 '89 to cellar)

Value Recommendations

Columbia Crest Cabernet Sauvignon
  Columbia Valley
Price Range $9–12
Preferred Vintages '88, '89

Monticello Cellars Cabernet Sauvignon
  'Jefferson Cuvée' *Napa Valley*
Price Range $9–12
Preferred Vintages '87, '88

Easy-to-Find or Alternative Selections

Robert Mondavi Winery Cabernet Sauvignon
  Napa Valley
Price Range $17–22
Preferred Vintages '87, '88

Hogue Cellars Cabernet Sauvignon
  Washington State
Price Range $11–14
Preferred Vintages '87, '88, '89

PRIME RIB OR STANDING RIB ROAST

Full bodied red wines are the rule to
match prime rib. The fatty nature of
this cut requires a wine with good
acidity and plenty of fruit. Washington
Merlot is fine, as are California Cabernet
Sauvignon and young red Burgundies
from the Côte d'Or in France.

Washington Merlot Producers

Woodward Canyon Winery *Washington*†
Andrew Will *Washington*†

Leonetti Cellar *Washington*†
Covey Run *Yakima Valley*
Hyatt Vineyards *Yakima Valley*†
Hogue Cellars *Washington State*
Look for Reserve
Price Range $10–22
Preferred Vintages '88, '89

California Cabernet Sauvignon Producers

Shafer Vineyards Napa Valley
Look for Hillside Select†
Smith-Madrone *Napa Valley*†
Streblow Vineyards *Napa Valley*†
William Hill *Napa Valley*
Burgess Cellars 'Vintage Select' *Napa Valley*
Alexander Valley Vineyards *Alexander Valley*
Arrowood Vineyards & Winery *Sonoma County*
Chalk Hills *Sonoma County*†
Price Range $15–30
Preferred Vintages '85, '86, '87

French Red Burgundy Producers

GEVREY-CHAMBERTIN
Louis Jadot
Domaine Maume†
Denis Bachelet†
Alain Burguet†
Look for Vieilles Vignes

NUITS-ST.-GEORGES
Mongeard-Mugneret†
Look for Les Boudots
Joseph Faiveley
Jules Belin†
Daniel Rion†

FIXIN
Clémancey Frères†
Price Range $22–40
Preferred Vintages '85, '87, '88, '89

Value Recommendation

Beaulieu Vineyards Cabernet Sauvignon
  'Beautour' *Napa Valley*
Price Range $9–12
Preferred Vintages '87, '88

Easy-to-Find or Alternative Selections

Fetzer Vineyards Cabernet Sauvignon 'Barrel
  Select' *California*
Price Range $10–14
Preferred Vintages '87, '88

Hogue Cellars Merlot *Washington State*
Price Range $9–12
Preferred Vintages '87, '88, '89

ROAST BEEF

The juice of medium-rare roast beef
smells a little like the aroma of well-
aged Bordeaux, particularly those from
the Graves commune. Since aged
Bordeaux can be expensive, I also
recommend California Cabernet
Sauvignon.

French Red Bordeaux Producers

Château Haut-Bailly *Pessac Léognan*
Château de Fieuzal *Pessac Léognan*†
Château La Louvière Rouge *Pessac Léognan*
Château Pape-Clément *Pessac Léognan*
Château La Mission-Haut-Brion *Pessac
  Léognan*†
Domaine de Chevalier *Pessac Léognan*†
Price Range $25–60
*Preferred Vintages '82, '85, '86, '87 ('88, '89
  to cellar)*

California Cabernet Sauvignon Producers

Laurel Glen *Sonoma Mountain*†
Livingston *Napa Valley*†
Grgich Hills Cellar *Napa Valley*
Beaulieu Vineyards *Napa Valley*
Look for Private Reserve 'Georges de Latour'
Jordan Vineyard & Winery *Alexander Valley*
Silver Oak Cellars *Alexander Valley*
Silver Oak Cellars *Napa Valley*†
Price Range $15–30
Preferred Vintages '85, '86 ('87 to cellar)

Value Recommendations

J. Pedroncelli Cabernet Sauvignon *Sonoma County*
Monticello Cellars Cabernet Sauvignon 'Jefferson Cuvée' *Napa Valley*
Price Range $9–12
Preferred Vintages '87, '88

Easy-to-Find or Alternative Selections

Beringer Vineyards Cabernet Sauvignon *Knight's Valley*
Price Range $10–14
Preferred Vintages '87, '88

Beaulieu Vineyards Cabernet Sauvignon 'Beautour' *Napa Valley*
Price Range $9–12
Preferred Vintages '87, '88

SHORT RIBS

With plenty of rosemary, black pepper, and onion, braised short ribs are the perfect companion to a bottle of French Côtes-du-Rhône Rouge or a good California Zinfandel.

French Côtes-du-Rhône Rouge Producers

E. Guigal
J. Vidal-Fleury
Château du Trignon
Kermit Lynch Selection
Price Range $7–12
Preferred Vintages '88, '89, '90

California Zinfandel Producers

Nalle *Sonoma County†*
Lytton Springs *Sonoma County*
Burgess Cellars *Napa Valley*
Ravenswood 'Vintner's Blend' *Sonoma*
Price Range $7–13
Preferred Vintages '87, '88, '89

Easy-to-Find or Alternative Selections

Sutter Home Zinfandel *California*
Price Range $5–8
Preferred Vintages '88, '89

La Vieille Ferme Côtes du Ventoux Rouge
Price Range $5–8
Preferred Vintages '88, '89, '90

TERIYAKI STEAK

The soy, garlic, and ginger of teriyaki
enliven the taste of the meat and call for
a big red Zinfandel or a bright, young
Bandol Rouge. A bottle of young
Beaujolais-Villages is also well suited to
the flavor of teriyaki steak.

California Zinfandel Producers

Lytton Springs *Sonoma County*
Storybook Mountain Vineyards *Napa Valley†*

Lamborn Family Vineyards 'Howell Mountain'
  Napa Valley†
Ridge Vineyards 'Geyserville'
Caymus Vineyards *Napa Valley*
Price Range $10–15
Preferred Vintages '87, '88, '89

French Bandol Rouge Producers

Château la Rouvière†
Domaine de l'Hermitage†
Domaine Tempier†
Look for La Tourtine
Domaine de Pibarnon†
Price Range $15–20
Preferred Vintages '85, '86, '87, '88

French Beaujolais-Villages Producers

Georges Duboeuf
Louis Jadot
Sylvain Fessy†
Louis Latour
Louis Trenel†
Price Range $7–10
Preferred Vintages '88, '89, '90

Easy-to-Find or Alternative Selection

Fetzer Vineyards Zinfandel 'Barrel Select'
  North Coast
Price Range $8–10
Preferred Vintages '88, '89

*L*AMB

The sweet flavor and mild texture of lamb are complemented by red wines, preferably well aged, with good balance and plenty of flavor.

LEG OF LAMB

The classic companion for roast leg of lamb is a bottle of aged French Bordeaux from the parish of Pomerol. But I prefer the new Italian red Vino da Tavola, many of which are blends of barrel-aged Sangiovese and Cabernet Sauvignon from Tuscany, especially if the meat is infused with garlic and herbs.

French Pomerol Producers

Château Clinet *Pomerol*
Château La Conseillante *Pomerol*
Château L'Église *Pomerol*
Château L'Évangile *Pomerol*
Château de Sales *Pomerol*
Price Range $20–45
*Preferred Vintages '82, '85, '86 ('88, '89 to
  cellar)*

Italian Red Vino da Tavola Producers

Fontodi 'Flaccianello'†
Fattoria di Felsina 'Fontalloro'†
L. Antinori 'Ornellaia'†

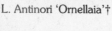

Castello di Rampolla 'Sammarco'†
Ruffino 'Cabreo'
Antinori 'Tignanello'†
Tenuta San Guido 'Sassicaia'†
Price Range $20–50
Preferred Vintages '85, '86, '88

Value Recommendation

Melini Chianti 'Borghi d'Elsa'
Price Range $5–8
Preferred Vintages '88, '89

Easy-to-Find or Alternative Selections

Beringer Vineyards Cabernet Sauvignon
   Knight's Valley
Price Range $10–14
Preferred Vintages '87, '88
Frescobaldi Chianti Classico
Price Range $5–8
Preferred Vintages '89, '90

RACK OF LAMB

A wide variety of red wines go very well
with rack of lamb. My preference is a
bottle of red Burgundy but well-aged
Bordeaux or Rhône Valley reds are also
great to serve.

French Red Burgundy Producers
CHAMBOLLE-MUSIGNY
Georges Roumier†
Domaine Dujac†
Comte de Vogüé†
Look for Les Amoureuses
Daniel Rion†

SAVIGNY-LES-BEAUNE
Tollot-Beaut†
Jean-Marc Pavelot†
Look for Aux Guettes

VOLNAY
Domaine de la Pousse d'Or†
Look for Bousse d'Or
Comte Lafon†
Look for Champans
Robert Ampeau†
Domaine Michel Lafarge†
Hubert de Montille†
Price Range $25–60
Preferred Vintages '85, '87 ('88, '89 to cellar)

French Red Bordeaux Producers

Château Gruaud Larose *St.-Julien*
Château Talbot *St.-Julien*
Château Beychevelle *St.-Julien*
Château Léoville-Las Cases *St.-Julien*
Château Rausan-Ségla *Margaux*
Château Bouscaut *Graves*
Château Sociando-Mallet *Haut-Médoc*
Price Range $20–45
Preferred Vintages '82, '85 ('86, '88, '89 to cellar)

French Red Rhône Valley Producers

Château du Trignon Côtes-du-Rhône Rouge
E. Guigal Côtes-du-Rhône Rouge
Domaine Les Pallières Gigondas†
Domaine Raspail-Aÿ Gigondas†
Kermit Lynch Selection Côtes-du-Rhône Rouge
Price Range $8–15
Preferred Vintages '85, '88, '89

Easy-to-Find or Alternative Selections

Louis Jadot Bourgogne Rouge
Joseph Drouhin Bourgogne Rouge 'Laforet'
Price Range $9–12
Preferred Vintages '88, '89

BRAISED LAMB SHANKS

The size of a lamb shank makes one think big when selecting a wine. Try an Italian Nebbiolo d'Alba or a Barbera d'Alba from a good producer.

Italian Nebbiolo d'Alba Producers

Montanello†
Ceretto
Bruno Giacosa
Giuseppe Mascarello
Prunotto
Franco Fiorina
Aldo Conterno
Price Range $12–18
Preferred Vintages '85, '86 ('88 to cellar)

Italian Barbera d'Alba Producers

Bruno Giacosa
Vietti†
Pelissero†
Clerico†
Angelo Gaja†
Giuseppe Rinaldi
Price Range $12–18
Preferred Vintages '88, '89

Easy-to-Find or Alternative Selection

Fontanafredda Nebbiolo d'Alba
Price Range $9–12
Preferred Vintages '88, '89

SKEWERED LAMB

Grilled or barbecued shish kebab or shashlik is a summertime favorite. Skewered lamb that has been marinated is wonderful when accompanied by California Zinfandel or Merlot. Also, the wine from Chateau Musar in Lebanon is an excellent match.

California Zinfandel Producers

Caymus Vineyards *Napa Valley*
Burgess Cellars *Napa Valley*
Preston Vineyards & Winery *Dry Creek Valley*
Ridge Vineyards *Howell Mountain*
Rafanelli Winery *Sonoma*†
Price Range $7–13
Preferred Vintages '87, '88, '89

California Merlot Producers

Clos du Val *Napa Valley*
Newton Vineyards *Napa Valley*
Rombauer Vineyards *Napa Valley*
Markham Winery *Napa Valley*
Cuvaison *Napa Valley*
Jaeger-Inglewood Vineyard *Napa Valley*†
Clos du Bois *Sonoma*
Rutherford Hill Winery *Napa Valley*
Price Range $12–20
Preferred Vintages '85, '87, '88

Lebanese Red Producer

Chateau Musar *Lebanon*†
Price Range $10–30
Preferred Vintages '78, '79, '82, '85

Easy-to-Find or Alternative Selections

J. Pedroncelli Zinfandel *Sonoma County*
Price Range $7–10
***Preferred Vintages** '87, '88*

Columbia Crest Merlot *Columbia Valley*
Price Range $9–12
***Preferred Vintages** '88, '89*

LAMB CURRY

The pungent, spicy elements of good curry make either a high-acid French white from the Rhône Valley or a Bandol rosé a perfect match. Crisp, young German Kabinett is a pleasant combination with lamb curry also.

French White Rhône Valley Producers

E. Guigal Côtes-du-Rhône Blanc
Domaine Desmeure St. Joseph Blanc†
Auguste Clape Côtes-du-Rhône Blanc†
Price Range $8–15
***Preferred Vintages** '89 '90*

French Bandol Rosé Producers

Moulin des Costes†
Domaine Tempier†
Château Vannières†
Domaine de L'Hermitage†
Price Range $12–18
***Preferred Vintages** '89 '90*

German Kabinett Producers

Selbach-Oster Zeltinger Himmelreich *Mosel*†
Dr. Loosen Erdener Treppchen *Mosel*†
Zilliken Saarburger Rausch *Saar*†

Weingut Georg Breuer Riesling Dry *Rheingau*†
Schloss Saarstein Serriger Schloss Saarsteiner
  Saar†
Von Schubert Maximin Grünhäuser Abtsberg
  Ruwer†
Price Range $12–18
Preferred Vintages '88, '89

Easy-to-Find or Alternative Selection
La Vieille Ferme Côtes du Lubéron Blanc
Price Range $5–8
Preferred Vintages '89, '90

LAMB STEW

The savory flavor of cubed lamb stewed
with tomatoes, onions, peas, turnips,
and potatoes is nicely matched by
medium-bodied red wines. Spanish
Rioja with a few years of bottle age,
young Chilean Cabernet Sauvignon, and
the hearty reds of the Côtes du
Roussillon region in France all go well
with lamb stew.

Spanish Red Rioja Producers

Berberana
Bodegas Olarra
La Rioja Alta
Marqués de Riscal
Bodegas Bretón 'Loriñón'†
Price Range $8–15
Preferred Vintages '85, '87, '88 ('89 to cellar)

Chilean Cabernet Sauvignon Producers

Cousiño-Macul *Maipo Valley*
Carta Vieja *Maule Valley*†

Los Vascos *Colchagua*
Undurraga *Maipo Valley*
Price Range $5–10
Preferred Vintages *'86, '87, '88*

French Côtes du Roussillon Producers

Caramany†
Domaine Guittard Rodor†
La Tour de France†
Château Cap de Fouste†
Domaine de Canterrane†
Château de Jau†
Price Range $8–13
Preferred Vintages *'86, '88, '89*

Easy to Find or Alternative Selections

Marqués de Cáceres *Rioja*
Price Range $6–10
Preferred Vintages *'85, '87, '88*

Santa Rita Cabernet Sauvignon *Maipo Valley, Chile*
Price Range $6–10
Preferred Vintages *'86 '87, '88*

MOUSSAKA

Great Spanish Rioja or Ribera del Duero reds are perfect with moussaka. An Italian Rosso di Montalcino is very appealing, too. Although they are often difficult to find, well-made Greek red wines also go nicely with moussaka.

Spanish Red Rioja Producers

Berberana
Bodegas Olarra
La Rioja Alta
Marqués de Riscal

Marqués de Cáceres
Bodegas Bretón 'Loriñón'†
Price Range $8–15
Preferred Vintages '85, '87, '88 ('89 to cellar)

Spanish Ribera del Duero Producers

Tinto Pesquera†
Balbás†
Viña Pedrosa†
Price Range $7–18
Preferred Vintages '85, '86 '88 ('89 to cellar)
(Additionally, the producer Bodegas Inviosa makes a wine called 'Lar de Barros' from grapes of the Extremadura region of Spain that is an excellent red wine worth seeking out. *Look for the '86 and '87 vintages.*)

Italian Rosso di Montalcino Producers

Tenuta Il Poggione
Lisini
Caparzo
Fattoria dei Barbi
Price Range $10–16
Preferred Vintages '87, '88 '89

Greek Red Wine Producers

Achaia Clauss 'Demestica'
Boutari
Château Carras
Price Range $8–12
Preferred Vintages '85, '87

Easy-to-Find or Alternative Selection

Torres 'Sangre de Toro' *Penedés*
Price Range $4–7
Preferred Vintages '87, '88

EAL

The delicate texture of veal and its complex flavor requires medium- to full-bodied red wines to enhance its taste without overwhelming its texture. Italian red wines are generally an excellent choice.

ROAST VEAL

The flavor of roast veal is rich yet delicate, so be sure that the red wine you choose has plenty of character. An Italian Brunello di Montalcino is excellent. Morellino di Scansano or full-flavored Valpolicella are also tasty with roast veal.

Italian Brunello di Montalcino Producers

Lisini
Caparzo
Canalicchio di Sopra†
Biondi Santi†
Tenuta Il Poggione
Price Range $20–50
Preferred Vintages '82, '83, '85

Italian Morellino di Scansano Producers

Sellari Franceschini†
Cantina Sociale di Morellino di Scansano†
Price Range $8–18
Preferred Vintages '83, '85, '88

Italian Valpolicella Producers

Le Ragose
Allegrini
Zonin
Price Range $8–15
Preferred Vintages *'88, '90*

Easy-to-Find or Alternative Selection

Masi Valpolicella
Price Range $7–10
Preferred Vintages *'88, '90*

SWEETBREADS

The complex taste of sweetbreads is
well complemented by Bourgogne
Rouge, Côte de Beaune Rouge, or
Oregon Pinot Noir.

French Bourgogne Rouge Producers

Robert Chevillon†
Leroy 'Bourgogne d'Avenay'†
Joseph Faiveley
Jean François Delorme†
Machard de Gramont†
Jean Tardy†
Price Range $10–18
Preferred Vintages *'88, '89, '90*

French Côte de Beaune Rouge Producers

BEAUNE
Joseph Drouhin
Look for Clos des Mouches
Daniel Sénard†
Tollot-Beaut†
Remoissenet†
Coron Père & Fils†

SAVIGNY-LES-BEAUNE
Jean-Marc Pavelot†
Look for aux Guettes
Antonin Guyon†
CORTON
Prince de Mérode†
Look for Bressandes
Louis Latour
Price Range $20–45
Preferred Vintages '85, '87, '88

Oregon Pinot Noir Producers

Adelsheim Vineyard *Willamette Valley*†
The Eyrie Vineyards *Willamette Valley*
Cameron Winery *Willamette Valley*†
Elk Cove Vineyards *Willamette Valley*
Look for Wind Hills Vineyard
Amity Vineyards *Oregon*†
Ponzi Vineyards *Oregon*
Price Range $10–18
Preferred Vintages '88, '89

Easy-to-Find or Alternative Selection

Louis Latour Bourgogne Rouge
Price Range $9–12
Preferred Vintages '88, '89

VEAL CHOPS

Veal chops are frequently stuffed, and
the ingredients of the stuffing must be
considered. In general, a bottle of
Chianti Classico will match most
preparations. The spicy, rustic flavor of
Montepulciano d'Abruzzo also
complements veal chops nicely.

Italian Chianti Classico Producers

Antinori Riserva
Monte Vertine†
Castello di Cacchiano†
Look for Riserva
Fontodi
Badia a Coltibuono
Price Range $8–25
Preferred Vintages '87, '88, '89

Italian Montepulciano d' Abruzzo Producers

Barone Cornacchia
Casal Thaulero
Valentini†
Price Range $8–22
Preferred Vintages '83, '85, '88

Easy-to-Find or Alternative Selections

Antinori 'Santa Christina'
Melini Chianti 'Borghi d'Elsa'
Price Range $5–8
Preferred Vintages '88, '89

VEAL MARSALA

The addition of Marsala gives scallops
of veal a unique flavor. The floral aroma
of Italian Arneis is a perfect match.
Softer reds such as Italian Chianti
are excellent.

Italian Arneis Producers

Bruno Giacosa†
Ceretto 'Blangé'†
Castello di Neive†
Price Range $12–20
Preferred Vintages '89, '90

Italian Chianti Producers

Castello di Ama
Gabbiano
Fattoria di Felsina
Fontodi
Castello di Fonterutoli
Selvapiana
Price Range $7–15
Preferred Vintages '87, '88, '89

Easy-to-Find or Alternative Selection

Frescobaldi Chianti Classico
Price Range $5–8
Preferred Vintages '89, '90

VEAL PICCATA

The lemon and capers of veal piccata
are nicely matched by French
Bourgogne Blanc and French
Savennières from the Loire Valley.

French Bourgogne Blanc Producers

Louis Jadot
Hervé Roumier†
A & P de Villaine
Chartron & Trébuchet
Bouchard Père & Fils
Price Range $10–18
Preferred Vintages '88, '89

French Savennières Producers

Domaine des Baumard†
Look for Clos du Papillon
Château d'Epiré†

Domaine du Closel†
Château de la Roche-aux-Moines†
Price Range $12–20
Preferred Vintages '88, '89

Easy-to-Find or Alternative Selection
Joseph Drouhin Bourgogne Blanc 'Laforet'
Price Range $9–12
Preferred Vintages '89, '90

OSSO BUCO

Osso buco is perhaps the most flavorful
way to prepare veal shanks and can
handle a hearty red wine. An Italian
Ghemme or Gattinara makes a nice
combination. Or try one of the new
Italian red Vino da Tavola wines from
Tuscany. Many are blends of Sangiovese
and Cabernet Sauvignon aged in
oak barrels.

Italian Ghemme Producers
Cantina Sociale di Sizzano e Ghemme†
Ponti†
Le Colline†
Rainoldi†
Vigneti di Cantalupo†
Price Range $10–15
Preferred Vintages '85, '86, '88

Italian Gattinara Producers
Nervi†
Luigi Ferrando

Vallana
Dessilani
Price Range $12–18
Preferred Vintages '85, '86, '88

Italian Red Vino da Tavola Producers

Fontodi 'Flaccianello'†
Fattoria di Felsina 'Fontalloro'†
L. Antinori 'Ornellaia'†
Castello di Rampolla 'Sammarco'†
Ruffino 'Cabreo'
Antinori 'Tignanello'†
Tenuta San Guido 'Sassicaia'†
Price Range $20–50 +
Preferred Vintages '85, '86, '88

Easy-to-Find or Alternative Selection

Fontanafredda Nebbiolo d'Alba
Price Range $9–12
Preferred Vintages '88, '89

SALTIMBOCCA

The flavors of prosciutto and sage
combine with veal to require full-
flavored red wines with a supple texture.
Try an Italian Brunello di Montalcino or
one of the new Italian red Vino da
Tavola wines from Tuscany. Many are
blends of Sangiovese and Cabernet
Sauvignon aged in oak barrels.

Italian Brunello di Montalcino Producers

Lisini
Caparzo
Canalicchio di Sopra†

Biondi Santi†
Tenuta Il Poggione
Price Range $20–50
Preferred Vintages '82, '83, '85

Italian Red Vino da Tavola Producers

Fontodi 'Flaccianello'†
Fattoria di Felsina 'Fontalloro'†
L. Antinori 'Ornellaia'†
Castello di Rampolla 'Sammarco'†
Ruffino 'Cabreo'
Antinori 'Tignanello'†
Tenuto San Guido 'Sassicaia'†
Price Range $20–50+
Preferred Vintages '85, '86, '88

Easy-to-Find or Alternative Selection

Frescobaldi Chianti Classico
Price Range $5–8
Preferred Vintages '89, '90

PORK

Most pork preparations are delicately flavored. Full-bodied whites and softer reds are the natural matches. Occasionally, a fully dry rosé also enhances the flavor of pork.

PORK CHOPS

Pork chops can be served plain or stuffed, and the stuffing usually features herbs or fruit, which won't overwhelm the taste of the meat. I prefer a big-style California Chardonnay or a California Pinot Noir. A bottle of young German Kabinett from the Mosel or Saar is a fine alternative.

California Chardonnay Producers

Chateau Montelena *Napa Valley*
Grgich Hills Cellars *Napa Valley*
Ferrari-Carano *Alexander Valley*†
Hess Collection *Napa Valley*
Trefethen Vineyards *Napa Valley*
Morgan Winery *Monterey*
Qupé *Santa Barbara County*†
Price Range $14–28
Preferred Vintages '88, '89, '90

California Pinot Noir Producers

Seghesio *Russian River Valley*
Saintsbury 'Garnet' *Carneros*

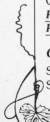

Carneros Creek 'Fleur de Carneros' *Carneros*
Bouchaine *Carneros*
Price Range $10–15
Preferred Vintages '88, '89, '90

German Kabinett Producers

Mönchhof Ürziger Würzgarten *Mosel*†
Zilliken Saarburger Rausch *Saar*†
Bert Simon Serriger Würtzberg *Saar*†
Milz Trittenheimer Felsenkopf *Mosel*†
Von Hövel Oberemmeler Hütte *Saar*†
Price Range $12–18
Preferred Vintages '88, '89

Easy-to-Find or Alternative Selection

Fetzer Vineyards Chardonnay 'Barrel Select'
  Mendocino
Price Range $9–12
Preferred Vintages '89, '90

PORK ROAST

The sweet yet dry taste of pork roast
makes it a candidate to be accompanied
by a bottle of California dry rosé or a
French Tavel rosé. For white wine, try a
dry Chenin Blanc from a respected
producer or a full-bodied California
Chardonnay.

California Dry Rosé Producers

Ridge Vineyards Carignan Rosé *Geyserville*
Heitz Cellars Grignolino Rosé *Napa Valley*
Bonny Doon Vineyard 'Vin Gris de Cigare'
  Santa Cruz
Price Range $8–12
Preferred Vintages (youngest available)

French Tavel Rosé Producers

Château d'Aqueria†
E. Guigal†
Domaine de la Forcadière†
Le Vieux Moulin†
Price Range $8–12
Preferred Vintages (youngest available)

California Dry Chenin Blanc Producers

Folie-à-Deux *Napa Valley*†
Girard Winery *Napa Valley*
Villa Mt. Eden Winery *Napa Valley*
Seghesio *Russian River Valley*
Guenoc Winery *Lake County*
Price Range $7–10
Preferred Vintages '89, '90

California Chardonnay Producers

Silverado Vineyards *Napa Valley*
Frog's Leap Wine Cellars *Napa Valley*
Matanzas Creek *Sonoma*
David Bruce *Sonoma-Mendocino*
Joseph Phelps Vineyards *Napa Valley*
Look for Sangiacomo
Price Range $13–20
Preferred Vintages '88, '89, '90

Easy-to-Find or Alternative Selections

Kenwood Vineyards Chardonnay *Sonoma
County*
Price Range $12–15
Preferred Vintages '89, '90

Robert Mondavi Winery Chardonnay *Napa
Valley*
Price Range $13–16
Preferred Vintages '88, '89, '90

PORK
TENDERLOIN

The succulence of a grilled pork
tenderloin is well complemented by
Pinot Noir. Try a bottle of Oregon Pinot
Noir or a Bourgogne Rouge.

Oregon Pinot Noir Producers

Adelsheim Vineyard *Willamette Valley*
The Eyrie Vineyards *Willamette Valley*
Cameron Winery *Willamette Valley†*
Amity Vineyards *Oregon†*
Price Range $10–18
Preferred Vintages '88, '89

French Bourgogne Rouge Producers

A & P de Villaine
Louis Jadot
Joseph Faiveley
Philippe Rossignol†
Price Range $10–18
Preferred Vintages '88, '89

Easy-to-Find or Alternative Selection

Joseph Drouhin Bourgogne Rouge 'Laforet'
Price Range $9–12
Preferred Vintages '88, '89

BARBECUED
SPARERIBS

Hot and spicy barbecued spareribs call
for a California Zinfandel or an
Australian Shiraz. The rare Lemberger
grape grown in Washington is also
savory with spareribs.

California Zinfandel Producers

Rafanelli Winery *Sonoma*†
Gundlach Bundschu *Sonoma*†
Ravenswood 'Vintner's Blend' *Sonoma*
Ridge Vineyards 'Lytton Springs' *Sonoma*
Clos du Val *Napa Valley*
Price Range $7–14
Preferred Vintages '87, '88, '89

Australian Shiraz Producers

Redbank *Victoria*†
Henschke *Eden Valley*†
Taltarni *Victoria*
Cassegrain *Southeastern Australia*†
Penfolds 'Bin 128' *Coonawarra*
Rosemount Estate *Hunter Valley*
Price Range $8–15
Preferred Vintages '86, '87, '89

Washington Lemberger Producers

Kiona Vineyards *Columbia Valley*†
Covey Run *Yakima Valley*†
Snoqualmie Winery *Washington*†
Price Range $7–12
Preferred Vintages '88, '89

Easy-to-Find or Alternative Selections

Round Hill Vineyards Zinfandel *California*
Price Range $7–10
Preferred Vintages '88, '89

Lindeman's Shiraz 'Bin 50' *Southeastern
  Australia*
Price Range $7–10
Preferred Vintages '87, '89

SAUSAGE:
KNOCKWURST, BRATWURST, AND FRANKFURTERS

For mild sausages, a bottle of Pinot Noir from France's Côte Chalonnaise is just the right match. Also, a good German Kabinett from the Mosel River valley is a nice complement. If these are hard to find, try an Oregon Pinot Noir.

French Côte Chalonnaise Producers
MERCUREY ROUGE
Daniel Chanzy†
Jean François Delorme†
Domaine Saier

GIVRY
Domaine Thénard†

BOURGOGNE ROUGE
A & P de Villaine
Vignerons de Buxy
Michel Juillot†
Price Range $10–18
Preferred Vintages '88, '89

German Mosel Kabinett Producers
Fritz Haag Brauneberger Juffer-Sonnenuhr *Mosel*†
Mönchhof Ürziger Würzgarten *Mosel*†
Dr. Loosen Erdener Treppchen *Mosel*†
Selbach-Oster Zeltinger Sonnenuhr *Mosel*†
Selbach-Oster Graacher Domprobst *Mosel*†
Price Range $8–15
Preferred Vintages '88, '89

Oregon Pinot Noir Producers

Adelsheim Vineyard *Oregon*†
The Eyrie Vineyards *Willamette Valley*
Sokol Blosser Winery 'Redland'
Bethel Heights Vineyard *Willamette Valley*†
Amity Vineyards *Oregon*†
Price Range $10–18
Preferred Vintages '88, '89

Easy-to-Find or Alternative Selection

La Vieille Ferme Côtes du Ventoux Rouge
Price Range $5–8
Preferred Vintages '88, '89, '90

HOT SAUSAGE: CHORIZO, ITALIAN, AND CREOLE

The heat of these sausages will
generally overwhelm almost any wine,
but a hearty red tastes refreshing as a
palate cleanser. Either a red wine from
France's Midi district or an Italian
Dolcetto is fine for this purpose.

French Corbières and Midi Producers

Domaine de Mont Tauch 'Fitou'†
Château de Ségure 'Fitou'†
Domaine de Fonsainte 'Corbières'†
Château de Paraza 'Minervois'†
Château Villerambert Julien 'Minervois'†
Gilbert Alquier 'Faugères'†
Château de Jau 'Côtes de Roussillon'†
Price Range $7–13
Preferred Vintages '88, '89

Italian Dolcetto d'Alba Producers

Cavallotto
Bruno Giacosa
Elvio Cogno†
Paulo Scavino
Berutti Pietro 'La Spinona'†
Pelissero†
Price Range $8–15
Preferred Vintages '88, '89

Easy-to-Find or Alternative Selection

La Vieille Ferme Côtes du Ventoux Rouge
Price Range $5–8
Preferred Vintages '88, '89, '90

BAKED HAM

Around the holidays, the number of
requests a wine merchant receives for a
wine to go with baked ham is
astonishing. Baked ham is both a
popular holiday meal and a difficult food
to match with wine. The classic wine to
serve is dry rosé, but a soft Pinot Noir
from California or Oregon is tasty with
mustard and clove preparations. A full-
flavored Chardonnay with plenty of oak
is well suited to honey-glazed ham as is
a floral Pinot Grigio from Italy. The
Beaujolais Nouveau is released in mid-
November and its youthful, fruity
taste is also a fine marriage
with baked ham.

California Rosé Producers

Heitz Cellars Grignolino Rosé *Napa Valley*
Ridge Vineyards Carignan Rosé *Geyserville*†
Simi Winery Rosé of Cabernet *Sonoma County*
Bonny Doon Vineyard 'Vin Gris de Cigare' *Santa Cruz*
Price Range $7–12
Preferred Vintages (youngest available)

California and Oregon Pinot Noir Producers

Saintsbury 'Garnet' *Carneros*
Carneros Creek 'Fleur de Carneros' *Carneros*
Barrow Green *California*
Adelsheim Vineyard *Oregon*†
The Eyrie Vineyards *Willamette Valley*
Price Range $9–18
Preferred Vintages '88 '89

California Chardonnay Producers

De Loach Vineyards *Sonoma County*
Kistler Vineyards *Sonoma*†
Look for Dutton Ranch, Kistler Estate
Simi Winery *Sonoma*
Cambria *Santa Maria Valley*†
Robert Talbott Vineyard *Monterey*†
Edna Valley Vineyard *Edna Valley*
Crichton Hall *Napa Valley*†
Price Range $10–25
Preferred Vintages '88, '89, '90

Italian Pinot Grigio Producers

Livio Felluga
Santa Margherita
Josef Brigl
Tiefenbrunner
Price Range $10–17
Preferred Vintages '89, '90

French Beaujolais Nouveau Producers

Georges Duboeuf
Bouchard Père & Fils
Sylvain Fessy†
Mommessin
Price Range $9–14
Preferred Vintages (only the current year)

Easy-to-Find or Alternative Selections

Kendall Jackson Chardonnay 'Vintner's
  Reserve' *California*
Price Range $10–14
Preferred Vintages '89, '90

Georges Duboeuf Beaujolais-Villages
Price Range $7–10
Preferred Vintages '89, '90

POULTRY

White wine is the standard for most poultry because the delicate flavor of the meat doesn't stand up well to the tannins of heavy red wine. But attention must be paid to the ingredients in any stuffing or sauce, as these can easily change a light flavor from soft to spicy, in which case a lighter red wine is recommended.

CHICKEN CORDON BLEU

Laced with thin slices of ham and cheese, Chicken Cordon Bleu turns simple chicken breasts into a complex flavor combination. The bright fruit of young Italian Pinot Grigio pairs with these flavors perfectly. The softer reds, like young French Beaujolais-Villages and Italian Valpolicella, are excellent with this dish as well.

Italian Pinot Grigio Producers

Tiefenbrunner
Santa Margherita
Borgo Conventi†
Gianni Vescovo
Price Range $10–17
Preferred Vintages '89, '90

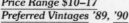

French Beaujolais-Villages Producers

Louis Jadot
Joseph Drouhin
Louis Latour
Louis Trenel†
Price Range $10–15
Preferred Vintages '88, '89, '90

Italian Valpolicella Producers

Masi
Look for Serègo Alighieri
Le Ragose
Allegrini
Price Range $8–15
Preferred Vintages '88, '90

Easy-to-Find or Alternative Selection

Georges Duboeuf Beaujolais-Villages
Price Range $7–10
Preferred Vintages '89, '90

CHICKEN KIEV

Butter and chives are the key flavors in
chicken Kiev. A bottle of full-flavored
California Chardonnay or a white
Burgundy from one of France's less-
expensive appellations is perfectly suited
to this dish.

California Chardonnay Producers

Dehlinger Winery *Sonoma*†
Edna Valley Vineyard *Edna Valley*
Acacia *Carneros*
Burgess Cellars *Napa Valley*
Trefethen Vineyards *Napa Valley*

Flora Springs *Napa Valley*
Freemark Abbey *Napa Valley*
Sonoma-Cutrer *Sonoma*†
Look for 'Les Pierres'
Grgich Hills Cellars *Napa Valley*
Price Range $13–25
Preferred Vintages '88, '89, '90

French White Burgundy Producers

SAVIGNY-LES-BEAUNE BLANC
Chartron & Trébuchet
Bitouzet†
Pierre Guillemot†

PERNAND-VERGELESSES BLANC
Michel Prunier†
Tollot-Beaut†
Antonin Guyon†
Louis Latour
Price Range $15–28
Preferred Vintages '88, '90

Value Recommendations

Kermit Lynch Selection Mâcon-Villages
Domaine Talmard Mâcon-Chardonnay
Price Range $10–14
Preferred Vintages '89, '90

Easy-to-Find or Alternative Selection

Kendall Jackson Chardonnay 'Vintner's
Reserve' *California*
Price Range $10–14
Preferred Vintages '89, '90

CHICKEN LIVERS
Earthy and sweet, chicken livers are
great sautéed with mushrooms and
onions. Try a bottle of Côtes-du-Rhône

Rouge or a Chinon Rouge. The strong flavors of good Côtes-du-Rhône Blanc wines from great vintages also stand up to the flavor of chicken livers.

French Côtes-du-Rhône Rouge Producers

Domaine de la Jasse†
Château St. Estève†
Paul Jaboulet-Aîné 'Parallèle 45'
Château du Trignon
Price Range $8–12
Preferred Vintages '88, '89, '90

French Chinon Rouge Producers

Charles Joguet†
Look for Clos de la Diotière
Olga Raffault†
Couly-Dutheil†
Look for Clos de l'Echo
Pierre-Jacques Druet†
Price Range $13–18
Preferred Vintages '88, '89

French Côtes-du-Rhône Blanc Producers

E. Guigal
Domaine du Mont-Redon
Auguste Clape†
Price Range $8–15
Preferred Vintages '89, '90

Easy-to-Find or Alternative Selection

E. Guigal Côtes-du-Rhône Rouge
Price Range $10–13
Preferred Vintages '88, '89

CHICKEN STEW OR POT PIE

This is basic fare that can be enlivened by a good bottle of wine. The peas, carrots, chicken, and cream sauce go nicely with Italian Orvieto Classico. Try a bottle of fruity young Beaujolais-Villages for a red wine to match chicken <u>pot pie</u>.

Italian Orvieto Classico Producers
Decugnano dei Barbi†
Bigi†
Look for Vigneto Torricella
Antinori
Barberani
Price Range $7–12
Preferred Vintages '89, '90

French Beaujolais-Villages Producers
Louis Jadot
Joseph Drouhin
Louis Latour
Price Range $10–15
Preferred Vintages '89, '90

Easy-to-Find or Alternative Selections
Ruffino Orvieto Classico
Price Range $7–10
Preferred Vintages '89, '90

Georges Duboeuf Beaujolais-Villages
Price Range $7–10
Preferred Vintages '89, '90

CHICKEN BREAST WITH TARRAGON

The cream and tarragon in this dish call for a white wine with good acidity and plenty of flavor. A bottle of dry white Bordeaux or Washington Sauvignon Blanc is ideal.

French White Bordeaux Producers

Château La Louvière *Pessac Léognan*
Château de Rochemorin *Graves*
Château Rahoul *Graves*†
Château Olivier *Pessac Léognan*
Château Couhins-Lurton *Graves*
Château Carbonnieux *Pessac Léognan*
Château La Garde *Martillac*
Château Magence *Graves*
Price Range $12–25
Preferred Vintages '88, '89

Washington Sauvignon Blanc Producers

Arbor Crest *Columbia Valley*†
Paul Thomas *Washington*†
Cavatappi Winery *Washington*†
Chateau Ste. Michelle *Columbia Valley*
Price Range $7–12
Preferred Vintages '89, '90

Easy-to-Find or Alternative Selection

Hogue Cellars Fumé Blanc *Washington State*
Price Range $7–10
Preferred Vintages '89, '90

COQ AU VIN

The origins of this classic meal mandate that it be served with a good French red table wine. France's Rhône Valley offers a large assortment of hearty reds that are wonderful with coq au vin.

French Côtes-du-Rhône Rouge Producers

J. Vidal-Fleury
Château du Trignon

Paul Jaboulet-Aîné 'Parallèle 45'
Château St.-Estève†
Price Range $7–15
Preferred Vintages '88, '89, '90

French Côtes du Ventoux Producers

La Vieille Ferme
Paul Jaboulet-Aîné
Price Range $5–8
Preferred Vintages '88, '89, '90

French Gigondas Producers

Domaine Raspail-Aÿ†
Domaine les Pallières†
Montmirail†
Price Range $14–18
Preferred Vintages '85, '86, '88, '89

Easy-to-Find or Alternative Selection

E. Guigal Côtes-du-Rhône Rouge
Price Range $10–13
Preferred Vintages '88, '89

FRIED CHICKEN

Surprisingly, red wines are the best
match for fried chicken. The
combination of oil and batter changes
the taste of the chicken from delicate to
meaty. I recommend full-flavored Italian
Chianti Classico or Chianti Rufina as
well as Spanish red Rioja.

Italian Chianti Classico Producers

Badia a Coltibuono
Monte Vertine†
Castello di Rampolla†

Fontodi
Castello di Fonterutoli
Fattoria di Felsina
Price Range $7–15
Preferred Vintages '87, '88, '89

Italian Chianti Rufina Producers

Selvapiana
Fattoria di Bossi
Frescobaldi 'Castello di Nipozzano'
Price Range $7–15
Preferred Vintages '87, '88, '89

Spanish Red Rioja Producers

La Rioja Alta
Berberana
Bodegas Bretón 'Loriñón'†
Marqués de Cáceres
Bodegas Olarra
Price Range $7–15
Preferred Vintages '85, '87, '88 ('89 to cellar)

Easy-to-Find or Alternative Selection

Frescobaldi Chianti Classico
Price Range $5–8
Preferred Vintages '89, '90

HERBED BAKED
CHICKEN

One can match almost any white wine,
save Chardonnay, with herbed baked
chicken; however, I prefer the crisp,
young style of Italian whites with this
meal. The dry whites of Orvieto are
fruity and fresh when young. The

stronger-flavored whites from Campania in southern Italy are full and rich and also go well with baked chicken. Or try a young Napa Valley Sauvignon Blanc.

Italian Orvieto Producers

Barberani
Look for Vallesanta
Decugnano dei Barbi†
Lamborghini†
Bigi†
Barbi
Price Range $7–12
Preferred Vintages '89, '90

Italian Campania Producers

Mastroberardino 'Fiano di Avellino'†
Struzziero 'Fiano de Avellino'†
Saviano 'Lacryma Christi'†
Mastroberardino 'Lacryma Christi'†
Mastroberardino 'Greco di Tufo'†
Price Range $9–14
Preferred Vintages '88, '89

California Sauvignon Blanc Producers

Cakebread Cellars *Napa Valley*
Robert Pepi *Napa Valley*
St. Clement Vineyard *Napa Valley*
Frog's Leap Wine Cellars *Napa Valley*
Honig Cellars *Napa Valley*
Price Range $8–15
Preferred Vintages '89, '90

Easy-to-Find or Alternative Selection

Antinori Orvieto Classico
Price Range $7–10
Preferred Vintages '89, '90

ROAST OR BROILED CHICKEN

Roast chicken is a versatile dish that goes well with many different types of wine. Lighter, dry whites, such as California dry Chenin Blanc, and medium-bodied reds are nice combinations. I personally prefer a bottle of Spanish red Rioja or a Ribera del Duero red with roast chicken because they are medium-bodied and yet, they are full-flavored. Or, look to the following sauces to determine your selection.

California Dry Chenin Blanc Producers

Folie-á-Deux *Napa Valley*†
Girard Winery *Napa Valley*
Villa Mt. Eden Winery *Napa Valley*
Pine Ridge Winery *Napa Valley*
Seghesio *Russian River Valley*
Price Range $7–10
Preferred Vintages '89, '90

Spanish Red Rioja Producers

Berberana
Bodegas Olarra
La Rioja Alta
Marqués de Riscal
Bodegas Bretón 'Loriñón'†
Price Range $8–15
Preferred Vintages '85, '87, '88 ('89 to cellar)

Spanish Ribera del Duero Producers

Tinto Pesquera†
Balbás†
Viña Pedrosa†
Price Range $7–18
Preferred Vintages '85, '86, '88 ('89 to cellar)
**(Additionally, the producer Bodegas Inviosa
makes a wine called 'Lar de Barros' from grapes
of the Estremadura region of Spain which is an
excellent red wine worth seeking out. *Look for
the '86 and '87 vintages.*)**

Easy-to-Find or Alternative Selection

Marqués de Cáceres *Rioja*
Price Range $10–13
Preferred Vintages '85, '87 '88

POULTRY SAUCES
MUSHROOM SAUCE

The earthy flavor of mushroom sauce
varies in intensity, depending on
whether the mushrooms are wild or
cultivated. For sauces with chanterelles,
morels, cèpes, or porcini, try a bottle of
Chianti Rufina or a Vino Nobile di
Montepulciano. For sauces made with
cultivated mushrooms, try an Italian
Chianti Classico.

Italian Chianti Rufina Producers

Selvapiana
Fattoria di Bossi
Frescobaldi 'Castello di Nipozzano'
Look for Montesodi
Price Range $7–15
Preferred Vintages '87, '88, '89

Italian Vino Nobile Producers

Avignonesi
Poderi Boscarelli
Podere Badelle†
Poliziano
Talosa
Price Range $14–20
Preferred Vintages '85, '86, '88

Italian Chianti Classico Producers

Fattoria di Felsina
Look for Riserva
Castello di Ama
Fontodi
Ruffino 'Riserva Ducale'
Isole e Olena
Price Range $8–15
Preferred Vintages '87, '88, '89

Easy-to-Find or Alternative Selection

Ruffino Chianti Classico
Price Range $5–8
Preferred Vintages '88, '89

FRUIT SAUCE

The tart, sweet flavor of sauces made with berries, currants, or plums is nicely matched by Oregon or California Pinot Noir. Also, a young Beaujolais-Villages complements this flavor.

Oregon Pinot Noir Producers

Sokol Blosser Winery 'Redland'†
Knudsen Erath Winery *Oregon*
Look for Vintage Select
Amity Vineyards *Oregon*†
Adelsheim Vineyard *Willamette Valley*†

Bethel Heights Vineyard *Oregon*†
Price Range $10–18
Preferred Vintages '88, '89

California Pinot Noir Producers

Saintsbury 'Garnet' *Carneros*
Bouchaine *Napa Valley*
Carneros Creek 'Fleur de Carneros' *Carneros*
Clos du Val *Napa Valley*
Price Range $7–15
Preferred Vintages '88, '89

French Beaujolais-Villages Producers

Sylvain Fessy†
Louis Jadot
Joseph Drouhin
Price Range $7–12
Preferred Vintages '88, '89, '90

Easy-to-Find or Alternative Selection

Georges Duboeuf Beaujolais-Villages
Price Range $7–10
Preferred Vintages '89, '90

TOMATO SAUCE

Classic preparations such as Chicken Cacciatore and Chicken Marengo use a tomato-based sauce that is nicely complemented by Italian reds. Try a Montepulciano d'Abruzzo or Chianti Rufina.

Italian Montepulciano d' Abruzzo Producers

Barone Cornacchia
Casal Thaulero
Valentini†
Price Range $8–22
Preferred Vintages '83, '85, '88

Italian Chianti Rufina Producers

Selvapiana
Fattoria di Bossi
Frescobaldi 'Castello di Nipozzano'
Look for Montesodi
Price Range $7–15
Preferred Vintages '87, '88, '89

Easy-to-Find or Alternative Selections

Antinori 'Santa Christina'
Melini Chianti 'Borghi d'Elsa'
Price Range $5–8
Preferred Vintages '88, '89

WINE SAUCE

When Madeira, Sherry, or Champagne is blended with cream, the result is a rich sauce that requires a bottle of French Bourgogne Blanc or Rouge with plenty of character.

French Bourgogne Blanc Producers

Louis Jadot
Hervé Roumier†
A & P de Villaine
Chartron & Trébuchet
Bouchard Père & Fils
Price Range $10–18
Preferred Vintages '88, '89

French Bourgogne Rouge Producers

A & P de Villaine
Louis Jadot
Joseph Faiveley
Philippe Rossignol†
Price Range $10–18
Preferred Vintages '88, '89

Easy-to-Find or Alternative Selection

Joseph Drouhin Bourgogne Blanc 'Laforet'
Price Range $9–12
Preferred Vintages '89, '90

TERIYAKI SAUCE

The soy, garlic, and ginger give Teriyaki a bright, salty flavor that marries well with California Zinfandel and French Beaujolais-Villages.

California Zinfandel Producers

Lytton Springs *Sonoma County*
Storybook Mountain Vineyards *Napa Valley*†
Burgess Cellars *Napa Valley*†
Ridge Vineyards 'Geyserville'
Caymus Vineyards *Napa Valley*
Price Range $10–15
Preferred Vintages '87, '88, '89

French Beaujolais-Villages Producers

Georges Duboeuf
Louis Jadot
Sylvain Fessy†
Louis Latour
Louis Trenel†
Price Range $7–10
Preferred Vintages '89, '90

Easy-to-Find or Alternative Selection

Fetzer Vineyards Zinfandel 'Barrel Select'
    North Coast
Price Range $8–10
Preferred Vintages '88, '89

BARBECUE SAUCE

Tomato, molasses, brown sugar, chili, and onion give barbecue sauce a tangy taste that is nicely matched by California Zinfandel and French Côtes-du-Rhône.

California Zinfandel Producers

Rafanelli Winery *Sonoma*†
Burgess Cellars *Napa Valley*
Marietta Cellars *Sonoma County*
Karly *Amador County*
De Loach Vineyards *Sonoma County*
Price Range $7–13
Preferred Vintages '87, '88, '89

French Côtes-du-Rhône Rouge Producers

J. Vidal-Fleury
Château du Trignon
Kermit Lynch Selection
Price Range $7–12
Preferred Vintages '88, '89, '90

Easy-to-Find or Alternative Selection

E. Guigal Côtes-du-Rhône Rouge
Price Range $10–13
Preferred Vintages '88, '89

ROAST GAME
HENS

The rich, sweet meat of roast Cornish game hens calls for medium-bodied reds such as Chianti Classico or Vino Nobile di Montepulciano.

Italian Chianti Classico Producers

Badia a Coltibuono
Monte Vertine†
Castello di Rampolla†
Fontodi

Castello di Fonterutoli
Antinori
Price Range $7–15
Preferred Vintages '87, '88, '89

Italian Vino Nobile Producers
Avignonesi
Poderi Boscarelli
Podere Badelle†
Poliziano
Talosa
Price Range $14–20
Preferred Vintages '85, '86, '88

Easy-to-Find or Alternative Selection
Ruffino Chianti Classico
Price Range $5–8
Preferred Vintages '88, '89

ROAST TURKEY

The traditional Thanksgiving meal is
one of the most difficult to match with
wine. Roast turkey, yams, cranberry
sauce, Brussels sprouts, and mashed
potatoes all have uniquely different
flavors. Off-dry whites such as Chenin
Blanc and dry white Riesling are
appealing and popular with most family
members. Pinot Noir and Beaujolais
also taste very good with this meal.
Look to the ingredients used in the
stuffings listed below to determine
which wine to serve.

TURKEY
STUFFINGS
ONION AND HERB
STUFFING

A stuffing of onions and herbs should
be matched with full-flavored California
Chardonnay or Bourgogne Blanc.

California Chardonnay Producers

Murphy-Goode *Alexander Valley*
Clos du Val *Carneros*
Silverado Vineyards *Napa Valley*
Sterling Vineyards *Napa Valley*
Price Range $12–18
Preferred Vintages '88, '89, '90

French Bourgogne Blanc Producers

Louis Jadot
Hervé Roumier†
A & P de Villaine
Chartron & Trébuchet
Bouchard Père & Fils
Price Range $10–18
Preferred Vintages '88, '89

Easy-to-Find or Alternative Selection

Kendall Jackson Chardonnay 'Vintner's
   Reserve' *California*
Price Range $10–14
Preferred Vintages '89, '90

APPLE OR PRUNE STUFFING

For apple or prune stuffing, dry Chenin Blanc or dry white Riesling is recommended. Vouvray with good acidity from one of the better producers is also excellent.

Washington Dry Chenin Blanc Producers

Covey Run *Yakima Valley*
Hogue Cellars *Washington State*
Chateau Ste. Michelle *Columbia Valley*
Snoqualmie Winery *Washington*
Price Range $5–8
Preferred Vintages '89, '90

California Dry White Riesling Producers

Trefethen Vineyards *Napa Valley*
Joseph Phelps Vineyards 'Early Harvest' *Napa Valley*
Price Range $7–12
Preferred Vintages '89, '90

French Vouvray Producers

Marc Brédif
Domaine Moriette†
Château Moncontour
Gaston Huet†
Price Range $8–15
Preferred Vintages '89, '90

Easy-to-Find or Alternative Selection

Monmousseau Vouvray
Price Range $8–15
Preferred Vintages '89, '90

OYSTER STUFFING

Washington Sauvignon Blanc and French Chablis are very good with oyster stuffing.

Washington Sauvignon Blanc Producers

Arbor Crest *Columbia Valley*†
Paul Thomas *Washington*†
Chinook *Washington*†
Chateau Ste. Michelle *Columbia Valley*
Price Range $7–12
Preferred Vintages '89, '90

French Chablis Producers

Bichot
René & Vincent Dauvissat
Louis Michel
Joseph Drouhin
Price Range $15–25
Preferred Vintages '88, '89

Easy-to-Find or Alternative Selection

Hogue Cellars Fumé Blanc *Washington State*
Price Range $7–10
Preferred Vintages '89, '90

CHESTNUT OR WALNUT STUFFING

Alsatian Rieslings or dry white Rieslings from Washington offer wonderful flavor combinations with walnut or chestnut stuffings. Good California Pinot Noirs and French Beaujolais-Villages are also very tasty.

Alsatian Riesling Producers

Gustave Lorentz
Hugel
F. E. Trimbach
Zind-Humbrecht
Price Range $8–15
Preferred Vintages '88, '89

Washington Dry White Riesling Producers

Chateau Ste. Michelle *Columbia Valley*
Hogue Cellars *Washington State*
Louis Facelli *Washington*†
Price Range $6–9
Preferred Vintages '89, '90

California Pinot Noir Producers

Saintsbury 'Garnet' *Carneros*
Bouchaine *Napa Valley*
Carneros Creek 'Fleur de Carneros' *Carneros*
Clos du Val *Napa Valley*
Price Range $7–15
Preferred Vintages '88, '89

French Beaujolais-Villages Producers

Sylvain Fessy†
Louis Jadot
Joseph Drouhin
Price Range $7–12
Preferred Vintages '88, '89, '90

Easy-to-Find or Alternative Selection

Georges Duboeuf Beaujolais-Villages
Price Range $7–10
Preferred Vintages '89, '90

SAUSAGE

Heavier reds go very nicely with the spices of sausage stuffing. Try a California Zinfandel.

California Zinfandel Producers

De Loach Vineyards *Sonoma County*
Caymus Vineyards *Napa Valley*
Burgess Cellars *Napa Valley*†
Round Hill Vineyards *California*
Price Range $7–13
Preferred Vintages '87, '88, '89

CRANBERRY AND RICE STUFFING

For cranberry and rice stuffing, Pinot Noirs from Burgundy are excellent.

French Bourgogne Rouge Producers

Joseph Faiveley
Joseph Drouhin
Mongeard-Mugneret†
Price Range $10–18
Preferred Vintages '88, '89

Easy-to-Find or Alternative Selection

Louis Latour Bourgogne Rouge
Price Range $9–12
Preferred Vintages '88, '89

GAME BIRDS

The unique flavors of the meats that fall under the classification of game birds have one common characteristic—intensity. Therefore, the red and white wines to match goose, quail, duck, pheasant, and squab should also be intense.

DUCK À L'ORANGE

The sweet citrus note of this gamey dish makes young Pinot Noir the perfect choice. California Pinot Noirs, which are full of berry and cherry flavors but have good balance, are ideal. Australian Pinot Noir is difficult to find but worth seeking out. Also young red Burgundies from the Côte de Beaune are excellent.

California Pinot Noir Producers

Au Bon Climat *Santa Barbara*†
Robert Mondavi Winery *Napa Valley*
Look for Reserve
Robert Stemmler Winery *Sonoma*†
Wild Horse Vineyards *Sonoma*†
Z-D *Napa Valley*†
Chalone Vineyards *Monterey*†
Acacia *Carneros*
Saintsbury *Carneros*
Price Range $15–25
Preferred Vintages '87, '88, '89

Australian Pinot Noir Producers

Mountadam *Eden Valley*†
Cold Stream Hills *Geelong*†
Wirra Wirra *McLaren Vale*†
Cullen's *Margaret River*†
Price Range $13–25
Preferred Vintages '85, '87, '89

French Côte de Beaune Rouge Producers

BEAUNE
Joseph Drouhin
Look for Clos des Mouches
Daniel Sénard†
Tollot-Beaut†
Remoissenet†
Coron Père & Fils†

SAVIGNY-LES-BEAUNE
Jean-Marc Pavelot †
Look for aux Guettes
Antonin Guyon†
Price Range $20–28
Preferred Vintages '87, '88, '89

Value Recommendations

Saintsbury Pinot Noir 'Garnet' *Carneros*
Seghesio Pinot Noir *Russian River Valley*
Mountain View Pinot Noir *California*
Price Range $7–10
Preferred Vintages '89, '90

Easy-to-Find or Alternative Selection

Robert Mondavi Winery Pinot Noir *Napa Valley*
Price Range $14–18
Preferred Vintages '88, '89

ROAST DUCK

Roast duck calls for red Burgundy from the Côte de Nuits or a great California

Pinot Noir if the accompanying sauce has a berry or Port base. If the preparation is Chinese, with a molasses glaze, or if the duck is served without a sauce, full-bodied Alsatian Gewürztraminer or Tokay Pinot Gris will go very nicely.

French Côte de Nuits Producers

MOREY-SAINT-DENIS
Domaine Dujac†
Look for Clos de la Roche
Georges Lignier†

CHAMBOLLE-MUSIGNY
Domaine Ponsot†
Georges Roumier†
Look for Les Amoureuses
Comte de Vogüé†
Look for Les Amoureuses

CLOS-DE-VOUGEOT
René Engel†
Mongeard-Mugneret†
Jadot 'L'Héritier Guyot'†
Joseph Faiueley
Price Range $40–75
Preferred Vintages '85, '87, '88, '89

California Pinot Noir Producers
Saintsbury *Carneros*
Calera *Central Coast*†
Look for Jensen
Au Bon Climat *Santa Barbara*†
Kent Rasmussen Winery *Carneros*†
Caymus Vineyards *Napa Valley*
Look for Special Selection
Price Range $10–22
Preferred Vintages '88, '89

Alsatian Gewürztraminer Producers

Zind-Humbrecht
Hugel
Marcel Diess†
Muré†
Look for Clos St. Landelin
Price Range $12–20
Preferred Vintages '88, '89

Alsatian Tokay Pinot Gris Producers

Hugel
Domaine Weinbach†
Zind-Humbrecht
Look for Clos Jebsal, Clos Windsbuhl†
Josmeyer
Dopff 'Au Moulin'
Price Range $9–20
Preferred Vintages '88, '89

Easy-to-Find or Alternative Selections

Robert Mondavi Winery Pinot Noir *Napa Valley*
Price Range $14–18
Preferred Vintages '88, '89

F. E. Trimbach Gewürztraminer
Price Range $9–12
Preferred Vintages '88, '89

ROAST GOOSE

To match the fatty nature of roast
goose, a powerful red wine is required.
The heady, aromatic wines from
France's Rhône Valley are excellent with
goose. Or a bottle of aged Barbaresco or
Nebbiolo d'Alba goes well with
this meal.

French Cornas Producers

Noel Verset†
Auguste Clape†
Marcel Juge†
Price Range $20–28
Preferred Vintages '85, '86, ('88, '89 to cellar)

French Côte-Rôtie Producers

E. Guigal
René Rostaing†
Look for Côte Blonde
Robert Jasmin†
Paul Jaboulet-Aîné
Look for Les Jumelles
Albert Dervieux†
Price Range $30–50
Preferred Vintages '85, '86 ('88, '89 to cellar)

Italian Barbaresco Producers

Angelo Gaja†
Vietti†
Robert Voerzio
Berutti Pietro 'La Spinona'†
Renatto Ratti
Bruno Giacosa
Produttori del Barbaresco
Price Range $25–55
Preferred Vintages '78, '82, '85 ('88 to cellar)

Italian Nebbiolo d'Alba Producers

Franco Fiorina
Fontanafredda
Prunotto
Montanello†
Vietti†
Look for San Michele
Ceretto
Price Range $10–16
Preferred Vintages '85, '86, '88

ROAST PHEASANT

I prefer red Burgundy with pheasant, but others may prefer aged red Bordeaux. In either case the wine should be at the top of its class and should possess firm acidity.

French Red Burgundy Producers

GEVREY-CHAMBERTIN
Philippe LeClerc†
Look for Combe aux Moines
Joseph Faiveley
Joseph Roty
Look for Charmes-Chambertin
Domaine Ponsot†
Look for Latricières-Chambertin
Louis Trapet†
Look for Chapelle-Chambertin
Louis Jadot
Price Range $35–70
***Preferred Vintages *'85, '87, '88, '89**

French Red Bordeaux Producers

Château Cos d'Estournel *St.-Estèphe*
Château Léoville-Las Cases *St.-Julien*
Château Canon *St.-Emilion*
Château Gruaud Larose *St.-Julien*
Château Sociando-Mallet *Haut-Médoc*
Château Latour *Pauillac*†
Château La Mission-Haut-Brion *Pessac Léognan*†

Price Range $25–125+
Preferred Vintages '70, '78, *'82*, '85, ('86, '88,
   '89 to cellar)

Value Recommendation
Saintsbury Pinot Noir 'Garnet' *Carneros*
Price Range $9–12
Preferred Vintages '89, *'90*

Easy-to-Find or Alternative Selection
Robert Mondavi Winery Cabernet Sauvignon
   Napa Valley
Price Range $17–22
Preferred Vintages '87, '88

ROAST QUAIL

The texture of roast quail is somewhat
delicate, yet the natural oils give it a
gamey taste. For unadorned
preparations, I like a bottle of young
white Burgundy. When the quail is
accompanied by fruit or Madeira sauce,
a bottle of red Burgundy is just right.
Also complementary are the Italian red
Vino da Tavola blends—the new style,
premium Tuscan reds. Many are blends
of Sangiovese and Cabernet Sauvignon
aged in small oak barrels.

French White Burgundy Producers
CHASSAGNE-MONTRACHET
Domaine Ramonet†
Look for Les Ruchottes
Michel Niellon†
Look for Les Vergers

Jean-Noël Gagnard†
Look for Les Caillerets
Jean-Marc Morey†

PULIGNY-MONTRACHET
Étienne Sauzet†
Look for Les Combettes, Les Referts
Domaine Leflaive†
Look for Les Pucelles, Clavaillon
Domaine Carillon†
Look for Les Perrières, Les Champs-Canet
Maison Jean Germain†
Look for Les Grands Champs, Les Champgains
Price Range $35–60
Preferred Vintages '86, '88, '89

French Red Burgundy Producers
BEAUNE
Joseph Drouhin
Look for Clos des Mouches
Daniel Sénard †
Tollot-Beaut†
Remoissenet†
Coron Père & Fils†
Price Range $28–55
Preferred Vintages '85, '87, '88

Italian Red Vino da Tavola Producers

Fontodi 'Flaccianello'†
Fattoria di Felsina 'Fontalloro'†
L. Antinori 'Ornellaia'†
Castello di Rampolla 'Sammarco'†
Ruffino 'Cabreo'
Antinori 'Tignanello'†
Tenuta San Guido 'Sassicaia'†
Price Range $20–50 +
Preferred Vintages '85, '86, '88

Value Recommendation
Saintsbury Pinot Noir 'Garnet' *Carneros*
Price Range $9–12
Preferred Vintages '89, '90

Easy-to-Find or Alternative Selections

Joseph Drouhin Bourgogne Blanc 'Laforet'
Price Range $9–12
Preferred Vintages *'89*, *'90*

Robert Mondavi Winery Pinot Noir *Napa Valley*
Price Range $14–18
Preferred Vintages *'88*, *'89*

ROAST SQUAB

With roast squab, one has an option of either white or red wines. The white wines should have medium to full body and good acidity. I suggest a bottle of Alsatian Riesling or a California Chardonnay. Red wines must be light and fruity. Try a Beaujolais from the commune of Moulin-à-Vent.

Alsatian Riesling Producers

F. E. Trimbach
Hugel
René Schmidt
Look for Schoenenbourg †
Zind-Humbrecht
Look for Brand†
Domaine Weinbach†
Look for Cuvée Théo
Price Range $8–18
Preferred Vintages *'88*, *'89*

California Chardonnay Producers

Murphy-Goode *Alexander Valley*
Clos du Val *Carneros*
Silverado Vineyards *Napa Valley*

Jepson *Mendocino*†
Sonoma Cutrer *Sonoma*†
Look for Russian River Ranches
Chateau Montelena *Napa Valley*
Gauer Estate Vineyard *Alexander Valley*†
Price Range $14–20
Preferred Vintages '88, '89, '90

French Moulin-à-Vent Producers

Louis Jadot
Diochon†
Look for Cuvée Vieilles Vignes
Paul Janin †
Jean Beaudet
Price Range $12–20
Preferred Vintages '88, '89

Easy-to-Find or Alternative Selections

F. E. Trimbach Riesling
Price Range $9–12
Preferred Vintages '88, '89

Georges Duboeuf Beaujolais-Villages
Price Range $7–10
Preferred Vintages '89, '90

GAME

Game requires full-flavored wines with firm acidity and good structure. Bold, young reds with plenty of fruit and tannin are well suited to the intense flavors of game.

RAGOUT OF RABBIT

A mainstay on the menus of many Italian restaurants, ragout of rabbit is well complemented by the fuller style of Barbaresco or a young Barbera. Also, a bottle of aged Gattinara is a fine match.

Italian Barbaresco Producers

Ceretto

Ca' Romé

Castello di Neive
Look for Santo Stefano

Bruno Giacosa
Look for Gallina di Neive, Santo Stefano

Angelo Gaja†
Look for Costa Russi, Sori Tilden

Renato Ratti

Produttori del Barbaresco
Look for Asili, Rabajà

Vietti†
Look for Rabajà

Price Range $15–50 +

 Preferred Vintages '82, '85 '88

Italian Barbera Producers

Bruno Giacosa
Aldo Conterno
Coppo
Look for Camp du Rouss†
Ceretto
Cogno-Marcarini†
Vietti†
Renato Ratti
Price Range $12–20
Preferred Vintages '88, '89

Italian Gattinara Producers

Travaglini
Vallana
Luigi Ferrando
Nervi†
Price Range $10–15
Preferred Vintages '85, '86, '88

Easy-to-Find or Alternative Selection

Franco Fiorina Barbera d'Alba
Price Range $9–12
Preferred Vintages '88, '89

VENISON STEAK OR ROAST VENISON

The gamey flavor of venison calls for a powerful red wine. The tastes of aged Châteauneuf-du-Pape and young California Zinfandel are different from each other, yet each is powerful enough to stand up to venison.

French Châteauneuf-du-Pape Producers

Château de la Gardine
Château de Beaucastel
Domaine du Vieux Télégraphe
Domaine de la Nerte†
Domaine de la Solitude†
Price Range $13–25
Preferred Vintages '83, '85, '86 ('88, '89 to
  cellar)

(Additionally, Château Rayas makes an
exceptionally rare and expensive Châteauneuf-
du-Pape that is extraordinary. It is worth both the
trouble to find and the price asked. Look for the
'85, '86 and '88 vintages.)

California Zinfandel Producers

Caymus Vineyards *Napa Valley*
Storybook Mountain Vineyards *Napa Valley*†
Sky Vineyards *Napa Valley*†
Dehlinger Winery *Sonoma*†
Lamborn Family Vineyards *Napa Valley*†
Preston Vineyards & Winery *Dry Creek Valley*
Price Range $8–15
Preferred Vintages '87, '88, '89

Easy-to-Find or Alternative Selection

Beringer Vineyards Zinfandel *Napa Valley*
Price Range $8–12
Preferred Vintages '87, '88

*F*ISH

*The types of fish and their preparations
range in taste from light and delicate to
intense, oily, and rich. These different
flavors and textures require different
wines. In general, the wines should be
white, but occasionally a rosé or light
red wine may be appropriate.*

BLACKENED FISH

The hot, spicy style of blackened
seafood is a challenge to match. The
intensity of the spice mixture
determines which wine to serve. In
general, white Bordeaux and California
Sauvignon Blanc are safe suggestions.
But the best pairing for blackened fish
is an Oregon Pinot Noir. The berry
flavors and slightly earthy quality stand
up to the intensity of this preparation.

French White Bordeaux Producers

Château Bonnet *Entre-Deux-Mers*
Château de Launay *Entre-Deux-Mers*
Château Raspide *Langon*
Château Ferrande *Castres*
Domaine Challon *Bordeaux*
Price Range $7–13
Preferred Vintages '88, '89, '90

California Sauvignon Blanc Producers

Caymus Vineyards *Napa Valley*
Chimney Rock *Napa Valley*†

Preston Vineyards & Winery 'Cuvée de Fumé'
  Dry Creek Valley
Beaulieu Vineyards *Napa Valley*
Price Range $7–12
Preferred Vintages '89, '90

Oregon Pinot Noir Producers

Sokol Blosser Winery 'Redland'†
Knudsen Erath Winery *Oregon*
Look for Vintage Select
Amity Vineyards *Oregon*†
Adelsheim Vineyard *Willamette Valley*†
Bethel Heights Vineyard *Willamette Valley*†
Price Range $10–18
Preferred Vintages '88, '89

Easy-to-Find or Alternative Selection

Kenwood Vineyards Sauvignon Blanc
  Sonoma County
Price Range $9–12
Preferred Vintages '89, '90

BLACK COD

The "game" of seafoods, Pacific black
cod is very oily and strongly flavored.
Whether served smoked, pan sautéed, or
grilled, it requires the strongest white
wines. White Rhône wines, Spanish
white wines, and Italian Campania
whites will all stand up to the intense
flavor of black cod.

French White Rhône Valley Producers

E. Guigal Côtes-du-Rhône Blanc
Domaine Desmeure St. Joseph Blanc†
Auguste Clape Côtes-du-Rhône Blanc†
Price Range $8–15
Preferred Vintages '89, '90

Spanish White Wine Producers

Torres *Penedés*
Look for Gran Viña Sol
Montecillo *Rioja*
Marqués de Cáceres *Rioja*
Labastida *Rioja*
Martinsancho Verdejo *Rueda†*
Price Range $7–15
***Preferred Vintages** '88, '89, '90*

Italian Campania Producers

Mastroberardino 'Fiano di Avellino'†
Struzziero 'Fiano de Avellino'†
Saviano 'Lacryma Christi'†
Mastroberardino 'Lacryma Christi'†
Mastroberardino 'Greco di Tufo'†
Price Range $9–18
***Preferred Vintages** '88, '89*

Easy-to-Find or Alternative Selection

La Vieille Ferme Côtes du Lubéron Blanc
Price Range $5–8
***Preferred Vintages** '89, '90*

ROCK OR LING
COD

Rock or ling cod is an oily fish that
requires special wines to counter its
intensity. Unlike most white fish, which
are well matched by the more delicate
white wines, cod, with its oily texture,
can turn a perfectly enjoyable Orvieto
sour. Crisp white Bordeaux, served

young and well chilled, goes nicely. A
strong Spanish white wine is a perfect
complement as is a Washington
Semillon.

French White Bordeaux Producers

Château La Louvière *Pessac Léognan*
Château de Fieuzal *Pessac Léognan*†
Château Malartic-Lagravière *Pessac Léognan*
Château Carbonnieux *Pessac Léognan*
Price Range $15–30
Preferred Vintages '88, '89

Spanish White Wine Producers

Torres *Penedès*
Look for Gran Viña Sol
Montecillo *Rioja*
Marqués de Cáceres *Rioja*
Labastida *Rioja*
Martinsancho Verdejo *Rueda*†
Price Range $7–15
Preferred Vintages '88, '89, '90

Washington Semillon Producers

Louis Facelli *Washington*†
Snoqualmie Winery *Washington*
L'Ecole #41 *Washington*†
Chateau Ste. Michelle *Columbia Valley*
Chinook 'Topaz' *Washington*†
Price Range $8–12
Preferred Vintages '88, '89, '90

Easy-to-Find or Alternative Selection

Columbia Winery Semillon *Columbia Valley*
Price Range $5–8
Preferred Vintages '89, '90

DEEP-FRIED CALAMARI

Deef-fried calamari is often served with an aïoli sauce, rich in garlic. The bright flavor and oily texture of the sauce call for crisp white wines. I recommend a bottle of French Sancerre or a California Sauvignon Blanc. For calamari served with a tomato-based sauce, try an Italian Orvieto Classico or Pinot Bianco.

French Sancerre Producers

Henri Bourgeois
Look for Côtes des Monts Damnés
Paul Cotat†
Look for La Grande Côte
Hippolyte Reverdy
Jean-Max Roger
Price Range $14–24
Preferred Vintages '89, '90

California Sauvignon Blanc Producers

Caymus Vineyards *Napa Valley*
Sterling Vineyards *Napa Valley*
Beaulieu Vineyards *Napa Valley*
Hanna Winery *Sonoma*†
Price Range $7–12
Preferred Vintages '89, '90

Italian Orvieto Classico Producers

Decugnano dei Barbi†
Bigi†
Barberani
Vincenzo Cotti
Price Range $7–12
Preferred Vintages '89, '90

Italian Pinot Bianco Producers

Livio Felluga
Josef Brigl
Tiefenbrunner
Borgo Conventi†
Jermann†
Price Range $9–16
Preferred Vintages '89, '90

Easy-to-Find Alternative Selections

Kenwood Vineyards Sauvignon Blanc
   Sonoma County
Price Range $9–12
Preferred Vintages '89, '90
Ruffino Orvieto Classico
Price Range $7–10
Preferred Vintages '89, '90

FLOUNDER

There are many preparations for
flounder, ranging from battered and pan
fried to baked in herbs and wine, but
the flavor of flounder is usually delicate.
Try a bottle of California Sauvignon
Blanc or experiment with the new
American dry Chenin Blancs that are
being made in Washington and
California.

California Sauvignon Blanc Producers

Babcock Vineyards *Santa Ynez Valley*
Sterling Vineyards *Napa Valley*
Mayacamus *Napa Valley*

Chateau Souverain *Sonoma*
Carmenet *Sonoma*
Price Range $7–12
Preferred Vintages '89, '90

American Dry Chenin Blanc Producers

Folie-à-Deux *Napa Valley*†
Girard Winery *Napa Valley*
Seghesio *Russian River Valley*
Snoqualmie Winery *Washington*
Guenoc Winery *Lake County*
Price Range $7–10
Preferred Vintages '89, '90

Easy-to-Find or Alternative Selection

Beringer Vineyards Sauvignon Blanc *Napa Valley*
Price Range $7–10
Preferred Vintages '89, '90

HALIBUT STEAKS

Fresh halibut steaks almost seem to have been designed for white Bordeaux. Whether the fish is poached, pan sautéed, or grilled, the flavors match perfectly. Pouilly-Fumé from France's Loire Valley is also very nice to have with halibut steaks.

French White Bordeaux Producers

Château La Louvière *Pessac Léognan*
Château de Fieuzal *Pessac Léognan*†
Château Malartic-Lagravière *Pessac Léognan*
Château Carbonnieux *Pessac Léognan*
Price Range $15–30
Preferred Vintages '88, '89

French Pouilly-Fumé Producers

J. M. Masson-Blondelet†
Look for Les Bascoins
Michel Redde
Dagueneau†
Paul Figeat
Pascal Jolivet
Price Range $14–20
Preferred Vintages '89, '90

Value Recommendations

Château Bonnet Blanc *Entre-Deux-Mers*
Maître d'Estournel *Bordeaux*
Price Range $7–10
Preferred Vintages '88, '89, '90

Easy-to-Find or Alternative Selection

Beaulieu Vineyards Fumé Blanc *Napa Valley*
Price Range $6–9
Preferred Vintages '89, '90

HALIBUT WITH
CREAM AND
CAPERS

In this preparation, the capers and cream broaden the range of wines that can be served. A bottle of French Sancerre or California Sauvignon Blanc goes nicely. I personally love the taste of French Savennières with this dish.

French Sancerre Producers

Henri Bourgeois
Look for Côtes des Monts Damnés

Paul Cotat†
Look for La Grande Côte
Hippolyte Reverdy
Jean-Max Roger
Look for Chêne Marchand
Price Range $14–24
Preferred Vintages '89, '90

California Sauvignon Blanc Producers

Frog's Leap Wine Cellars *Napa Valley*†
Ferrari-Carano *Sonoma County*
Simi Winery *Sonoma County*†
Benziger *Sonoma*
Grgich Hills Cellars *Napa Valley*
Price Range $8–15
Preferred Vintages '89, '90

French Savennières Producers

Domaine des Baumard†
Look for Clos du Papillon
Château d'Epiré†
Domaine du Closel†
Château de la Roche-aux-Moines†
Price Range $12–20
Preferred Vintages '88, '89

Easy-to-Find or Alternative Selection

Kenwood Vineyards Sauvignon Blanc
    Sonoma County
Price Range $9–12
Preferred Vintages '89, '90

MAHI MAHI

Mahi mahi has a firm texture and
lovely flavor that complement the taste
of Italian Pinot Grigio and Oregon Pinot

Gris beautifully. French Pouilly-Fumé serves as a savory alternative with <u>mahi mahi.</u>

Italian Pinot Grigio Producers

Livio Felluga
Gianni Vescovo
Bollini
Josef Brigl
Borgo Conventi†
Price Range $10–17
Preferred Vintages '89, '90

Oregon Pinot Gris Producers

Adelsheim Vineyard *Oregon*†
The Eyrie Vineyards *Willamette Valley*
Ponzi Vineyards *Oregon*†
Rex Hill Vineyards *Oregon*†
Price Range $9–14
Preferred Vintages '89, '90

French Pouilly-Fumé Producers

J. M. Masson-Blondelet†
Look for Les Bascoins
Dagueneau†
Michel Redde
Pascal Jolivet
Price Range $14–20
Preferred Vintages '89, '90

Easy-to-Find or Alternative Selection

Santa Margherita Pinot Grigio
Price Range $14–17
Preferred Vintages '89, '90

RED SNAPPER
AND PERCH

The bright flavor and soft texture of red snapper and perch call for dry white wines such as California Sauvignon Blanc. My preference is a bottle of French Bandol rosé, which has firm acidity.

California Sauvignon Blanc Producers

Caymus Vineyards *Napa Valley*
Frog's Leap Wine Cellars *Napa Valley*
Benziger *Sonoma*
Iron Horse Ranch & Vineyards *Sonoma*
Price Range $8–15
Preferred Vintages '89, '90

French Bandol Rosé Producers

Moulin des Costes†
Domaine Tempier†
Château Vannières†
Domaine de Pibarnon†
Price Range $12–18
Preferred Vintages '89, '90

Easy-to-Find or Alternative Selection

Kenwood Vineyards Sauvignon Blanc
   Sonoma County
Price Range $9–12
Preferred Vintages '89, '90

BROILED OR
GRILLED SALMON

The texture of grilled salmon is denser than that of poached or baked salmon and is meaty enough to stand up to Pinot Noirs from Oregon or California. The cherry-like flavor of Pinot Noir goes especially well with grilled salmon, but white wines also taste good if they have very full body and firm acidity. California Chardonnays are the favorite choice, but big Australian Chardonnays are also recommended.

Oregon Pinot Noir Producers

Tyee Cellars *Willamette Valley*†
Bethel Heights Vineyards *Willamette Valley*†
Adelsheim Vineyard *Willamette Valley*†
Tualatin Vineyards *Willamette Valley*
The Eyrie Vineyards *Willamette Valley*
Price Range $10–18
Preferred Vintages '88, '89
(Domaine Drouhin, the Oregon Vineyard purchased by Robert Drouhin, the director of the well-respected French Burgundy négociant firm Joseph Drouhin, produces an excellent Pinot Noir. Look for the '88 and '89 vintages.)

California Pinot Noir Producers

Saintsbury 'Garnet' *Carneros*
Barrow Green *California*†
Kent Rasmussen Winery *Carneros*†
Caymus Vineyards *Napa Valley*
Look for Special Selection
Price Range $10–22
Preferred Vintages '88, '89

California Chardonnay Producers

Kistler Vineyards *Sonoma*†
Look for Kistler Estate
Chalone Vineyards *Monterey*†

Morgan Winery *Monterey*
Babcock Vineyards *Santa Ynez Valley*
Look for Grand Reserve†
Far Niente *Napa Valley*†
Patz & Hall *Napa Valley*†
Hess Collection *Napa Valley*†
Grgich Hills Cellars *Napa Valley*
Price Range $13–23
Preferred Vintages '88, '89, '90

Australian Chardonnay Producers

Wyndham Estate *Southeastern Australia*
Mountadam *Eden Valley*†
Rothbury Estate *Hunter Valley*
Look for Brokenback Vineyard
Cassegrain *Southeastern Australia*†
Look for Fromenteau Vineyard
Price Range $12–24
Preferred Vintages '87, '89, '90
(Mitchelton Vintners produces a varietal bottling of Marsanne from grapes grown in the Goulburn Valley in Australia. Aged in wood, this Marsanne has a unique flavor that marries well with broiled or grilled salmon.)

Value Recommendations

Seghesio Pinot Noir *Russian River Valley*
Price Range $7–10
Preferred Vintages '88, '89

Lindeman's Chardonnay 'Bin 65'
    Southeastern Australia
Price Range $6–9
Preferred Vintage '90

Easy-to-Find or Alternative Selection

Robert Mondavi Winery Chardonnay *Napa Valley*
Price Range $13–16
Preferred Vintages '88, '89, '90

POACHED SALMON WITH LEMON AND DILL

The taste of salmon poached in wine with lemon and dill is uniquely suited to the Chardonnays from California's Carneros district. When poached, the delicate flavors of the salmon are highlighted and require Chardonnays with good body and cleansing acidity. Washington Chardonnays are also appealing. For a different combination, try a sparkling wine from the Northwest.

California Chardonnay Producers

Saintsbury *Carneros*
Neyers *Napa Valley*
Hanzell *Napa Valley*†
Acacia *Carneros*
Look for Marina Vineyard
Sterling Vineyards *Carneros*
Look for Winery Lake
Bouchaine *Carneros*
Thomas Fogarty *Santa Cruz*
Price Range $12–25
Preferred Vintages '88, '89, '90

Washington Chardonnay Producers

Mt. Baker Vineyards *Washington*†
Silver Lake *Columbia Valley*†
Look for Reserve
Stewart Vineyards *Yakima Valley*†

Bonair *Yakima Valley*†
Chinook *Washington*†
Waterbrook *Washington*†
Woodward Canyon Winery *Columbia Valley*
Look for Roza Bergé
Covey Run *Yakima Valley*
Price Range $10–20
Preferred Vintages '88, '89, '90

Northwest Sparkling Wine Producers

Argyle Brut *Oregon*†
Whittlesey-Mark Brut *Oregon*†
Hogue Cellars Brut *Yakima Valley*†
Domaine Ste. Michelle Champagne Brut
    Washington State
Price Range $10–20

Easy-to-Find or Alternative Selections

Clos du Val Chardonnay *Carneros*
Price Range $13–16
Preferred Vintages '89, '90

Hogue Cellars Chardonnay Reserve
    Washington State
Price Range $10–14
Preferred Vintages '89, '90

SALMON MOUSSE
OR PÂTÉ

The flavor of salmon becomes less
intense in a mousse or pâté. Try a bottle
of good Mâcon-Villages or an Oregon
Chardonnay well chilled.

French Mâcon-Villages Producers

Jean Thévenot†
Look for Mâcon-Clessé

Domaine Talmard
Domaine Emilian Gillet†
Look for Mâcon-Clessé
Pierres Blanches
Manciat-Poncet†
Look for Mâcon-Charnay
Price Range $10–15
Preferred Vintages '89, '90

Oregon Chardonnay Producers

The Eyrie Vineyards *Willamette Valley*
Adelsheim Vineyard *Willamette Valley*†
Cameron Winery *Willamette Valley*†
Tualatin Vineyards *Willamette Valley*
Look for Reserve
Bethel Heights Vineyard *Willamette Valley*
Tyee Wine Cellars *Oregon*†
Price Range $12–22
Preferred Vintages '88, '89, '90

Easy-to-Find or Alternative Selection

Louis Jadot Mâcon-Villages
Price Range $10–14
Preferred Vintages '89, '90

SMOKED SALMON

Two types of smoked salmon are available. For salmon such as lox, smoked using a cold smoking process and moist in nature, a great combination is French white Graves. Smoked salmon that is cooked in a hot smoker has a drier texture and is excellent with Oregon Pinot Gris.

French White Graves Producers

Château La Louvière *Pessac Léognan*
Château de Fieuzal *Pessac Léognan*†
Château Malartic-Lagravière *Pessac Léognan*
Château Carbonnieux *Pessac Léognan*
Château Graville-Lacoste *Graves*
Price Range $15–30
Preferred Vintages '88, '89

Oregon Pinot Gris Producers

The Eyrie Vineyards *Willamette Valley*†
Adelsheim Vineyard *Oregon*†
Rex Hill Vineyards *Oregon*†
Ponzi Vineyards *Oregon*†
Price Range $9–14
Preferred Vintages '89, '90

Easy-to-Find or Alternative Selection

Kenwood Vineyards Sauvignon Blanc
   Sonoma County
Price Range $9–12
Preferred Vintages '89, '90

SEA BASS

Sea bass is usually prepared with a stuffing. The ingredients in the stuffing must be considered when determining which wines to serve. Generally, a white wine with bright flavor and a lingering finish will go with most preparations. Try a bottle of Oregon Pinot Gris or a Washington Semillon. Also, either Italian Vernaccia di San Gimignano or French Bandol rosé is a nice complement to sea bass.

Oregon Pinot Gris Producers

The Eyrie Vineyards *Willamette Valley*
Adelsheim Vineyard *Oregon*†
Rex Hill Vineyards *Oregon*†
Ponzi Vineyards *Oregon*†
Price Range $9–14
Preferred Vintages '89, '90

Washington Semillon Producers

Snoqualmie Winery *Washington*
Arbor Crest *Columbia Valley*†
Louis Facelli *Washington*†
Chateau Ste. Michelle *Columbia Valley*
Chinook 'Topaz' *Washington*†
Price Range $8–12
Preferred Vintages '88, '89, '90

Italian Vernaccia Producers

Teruzzi & Puthod
Look for Terre di Tufo†
Falchini
San Quirico
Giannina
Price Range $7–18
Preferred Vintages '88, '89, '90

French Bandol Rosé Producers

Moulin des Costes†
Domaine Tempier†
Château Vannières†
Price Range $12–18
Preferred Vintages '89, '90

Easy-to-Find or Alternative Selection

Hogue Cellars Semillon *Washington State*
Price Range $5–8
Preferred Vintages '89, '90

SEVICHE

The acidity of the marinade used to prepare seviche limits the number of wines that match its flavor. Dry white Graves and California Sauvignon Blanc are my first choices, but Italian Gavi is also excellent.

French White Graves Producers

Château La Louvière *Pessac Léognan*
Château de Fieuzal *Pessac Léognan*†
Château Malartic-Lagravière *Pessac Léognan*
Château Carbonnieux *Pessac Léognan*
Price Range $15–30
Preferred Vintages '88, '89

California Sauvignon Blanc Producers

Spottswoode Vineyard & Winery *Napa Valley*†
Caymus Vineyards *Napa Valley*
Ferrari-Carano *Sonoma County*
Sterling Vineyards *Napa Valley*
Benziger *Sonoma*
Price Range $8–15
Preferred Vintages '89, '90

Italian Gavi Producers

Fausto Gemme 'La Merlina'
La Scolca 'Gavi dei Gavi'
La Battistina
Granduca
Price Range $12–20
Preferred Vintages '89, '90

Easy-to-Find or Alternative Selection

Kenwood Vineyards Sauvignon Blanc
    Sonoma County
Price Range $9–12
Preferred Vintages '89, '90

FILET OF SOLE AMANDINE

The flavors of almond and sole blend well with herbal, young Sauvignon Blanc and dry white Bordeaux. For an unusual treat, try a glass of chilled Spanish Manzanilla Sherry.

California Sauvignon Blanc Producers

Babcock Vineyards *Santa Ynez Valley*
St. Clement Vineyard *Napa Valley*
Mayacamus *Napa Valley*
Chateau Souverain *Sonoma*
Chimney Rock *Napa Valley*†
Price Range $7–12
Preferred Vintages '89, '90

French White Bordeaux Producers

Château La Garde *Martillac*
Domaine La Grave *Graves*†
Château Magence *Graves*
Château Respide-Medeville *Graves*
Château Ferrande *Castres*
Price Range $10–15
Preferred Vintages '88, '89, '90

Spanish Manzanilla Sherry Producers

Hidalgo 'La Gitana'
Osborne
Barbadillo†
Emilio Lustau
Look for Almacenista Reserva
Price Range $7–15

Easy-to-Find or Alternative Selection

Kenwood Vineyards Sauvignon Blanc
  Sonoma County
Price Range $9–12
***Preferred Vintages** '89, '90*

DOVER OR PETRALE SOLE

Dover or Petrale sole has a very mild
taste. The side dishes to accompany this
meal should be considered when
selecting the wine. Usually an Italian
Orvieto Classico or a lighter Italian Gavi
goes nicely with sole. French Muscadet
is also pleasant.

Italian Orvieto Classico Producers

Decugnano dei Barbi†
Bigi†
Barberani
Vincenzo Cotti
Price Range $7–12
***Preferred Vintages** '89, '90*

Italian Gavi Producers

Fausto Gemme 'La Merlina'
La Scolca 'Gavi dei Gavi'
La Battistina
Granduca
Price Range $12–20
***Preferred Vintages** '89, '90*

French Muscadet Producers

Château de Chasseloir
Château de la Noë

Louis Métaireau
Look for Cuvée One†
Château de la Ragotière
Marquis de Goulaine
Price Range $8–15
Preferred Vintages '89, '90

Easy-to-Find or Alternative Selection

Antinori Orvieto Classico
Price Range $7–10
Preferred Vintages '89, '90

SWORDFISH

The steak of the seafood world,
swordfish requires firm and full-flavored
whites or medium-tannin reds. The
style of French Sancerre as well as that
of Chinon Rouge go nicely. Oregon
Pinot Noir with some bottle age also
tastes fine with swordfish.

French Sancerre Producers

Henri Bourgeois
Look for Côtes des Monts Damnés
Paul Cotat†
Look for La Grande Côte
Hippolyte Reverdy
Price Range $14–24
Preferred Vintages '89, '90

French Chinon Rouge Producers

Charles Joguet†
Look for Clos de la Diotière
Couly-Dutheil†
Look for Clos de l'Echo

Olga Raffault†
Beaudry†
Price Range $12–20
Preferred Vintages '88, '89

Oregon Pinot Noir Producers

Adelsheim Vineyard *Willamette Valley*†
Amity Vineyards *Oregon*†
The Eyrie Vineyards *Willamette Valley*
Ponzi Vineyards *Oregon*†
Price Range $10–18
Preferred Vintages '88, '89

Easy-to-Find or Alternative Selection

Comte Lafon Sancerre
Price Range $17–20
Preferred Vintages '89, '90

TROUT

The delicate flavor of rainbow or brook
trout is complemented by light, crisp
whites such as French white Bordeaux
or Italian Pinot Bianco from Friuli.
Young French Bandol Blanc also nicely
matches the flavor of trout.

French White Bordeaux Producers

Château Bonnet Blanc *Entre-Deux-Mers*
Château de Launay *Entre-Deux-Mers*
Château Reynier *Entre-Deux-Mers*
Château La France *Entre-Deux-Mers*
Price Range $7–13
Preferred Vintages '88, '89, '90

Italian Pinot Bianco Producers

Livio Felluga
Gianni Vescovo
Borgo Conventi†
Jermann†
Price Range $9–16
Preferred Vintages '89, '90

French Bandol Blanc Producers

Château Vannières†
Domaine de l'Hermitage†
Domaine de Pibarnon†
Price Range $14–18
Preferred Vintages '89, '90

Easy-to-Find or Alternative Selection

Santa Margherita Pinot Grigio
Price Range $14–17
Preferred Vintages '89, '90

GRILLED TUNA

The unique, meaty flavor of grilled tuna
marries well with a variety of wines.
Young California Chardonnay and
French Mâcon-Villages are nice
matches. The softer California Pinot
Noirs are also appealing with
grilled tuna.

California Chardonnay Producers

St. Andrews Winery *Napa Valley*
Clos du Val *Carneros*
Sonoma-Cutrer *Sonoma*†
Look for Russian River Ranches
Barrow Green *California*†
Price Range $10–15
Preferred Vintages '88, '89, '90

French Mâcon-Villages Producers

Domaine Talmard
J.J. Vincent
Louis Latour
Manciat-Poncet†
Caves de Prissé†
Price Range $10–15
Preferred Vintages '88, '89, '90

California Pinot Noir Producers

Barrow Green *California*
Saintsbury 'Garnet' *Carneros*
Dehlinger Winery *Sonoma*†
Étude *Napa Valley*†
Carneros Creek 'Fleur de Carneros' *Carneros*
Price Range $10–15
Preferred Vintages '88, '89

Easy-to-Find or Alternative Selection

Joseph Drouhin Mâcon-Villages
Price Range $10–14
Preferred Vintages '89, '90

SHELLFISH

Each type of shellfish is unique in flavor. For the most part, white wines are appropriate, but with certain preparations softer, fruity reds may enhance the flavor of the meal.

BOUILLABAISSE

Saffron and tomato are the key ingredients of a classic bouillabaisse. Good dry white Bordeaux and softer reds such as Pinot Noir and Côtes du Roussillon wines are all good suggestions.

French White Bordeaux Producers

Château Malartic-Lagravière *Pessac Léognan*
Château de Fieuzal *Pessac Léognan*†
Château La Louvière *Pessac Léognan*
Château Rahoul *Graves*†
Château Carbonnieux *Pessac Léognan*
Château de Rochemorin *Graves*
Price Range $15–35
Preferred Vintages '88, '89

California Pinot Noir Producers

Saintsbury 'Garnet' *Carneros*
Carneros Creek 'Fleur de Carneros' *Carneros*
Dehlinger Winery *Sonoma*†
Robert Mondavi Winery *Napa Valley*

 Look for Reserve

Caymus Vineyards *Napa Valley*
Look for Special Selection
Étude *Napa Valley*†
Price Range $10–22
Preferred Vintages '88, '89

French Côtes-du-Roussillon Producers

Caramany†
La Tour de France†
Château Cap de Fouste†
Domaine de Canterrane†
Château de Jau†
Price Range $8–13
Preferred Vintages '88, '89

Easy-to-Find or Alternative Selection

Maître d'Estournel *Bordeaux*
Price Range $7–10
Preferred Vintages '88, '89, '90

CIOPPINO

The spicy flavor of cioppino can be
paired with full-flavored whites having
good acidity or with Tuscan reds. I
recommend a bottle of Italian Gavi or
Vernaccia di San Gimignano for white
and Italian Chianti Classico or Chianti
Rufina for the red.

Italian Gavi Producers

Fausto Gemme 'La Merlina'
La Scolca 'Gavi dei Gavi'
La Battistina
Granduca
Price Range $12–20
Preferred Vintages '89, '90

Italian Vernaccia Producers

Teruzzi & Puthod
Look for Terre di Tufo†
Falchini
San Quirico
Giannina
Price Range $7–18
Preferred Vintages '89, '90

Italian Chianti Classico Producers

Fontodi
Fattoria di Felsina
Castello di Fonterutoli
Castello di Cacchiano†
Look for Riserva
Price Range $8–15
Preferred Vintages '87, '88, '89

Italian Chianti Rufina Producers

Frescobaldi 'Castello di Nipozzano'
Look for Montesodi
Selvapiana
Travignoli†
Fattoria di Bossi†
Fattoria di Vetrice
Price Range $8–18
Preferred Vintages '87, '88, '89

Easy-to-Find or Alternative Selection

Ruffino Chianti Classico
Price Range $5–8
Preferred Vintages '88, '89

CLAM CHOWDER
NEW ENGLAND
STYLE

A rich, creamy, New England–style
clam chowder is complemented by the

pure clean Chardonnay flavor of a young French Mâcon-Villages. Spicy Italian Pinot Grigio and Alsatian Tokay Pinot Gris are nice combinations too.

French Mâcon-Villages Producers

J. J. Vincent
Domaine Talmard
Georges Duboeuf
Kermit Lynch Selection
Guffens-Heynen
Jean Thévenot †
Look for Mâcon-Clessé
Price Range $10–15
Preferred Vintages '88, '89

Italian Pinot Grigio Producers

Livio Felluga
Jermann†
Gianni Vescovo
Santa Margherita
Plozner
Price Range $10–17
Preferred Vintages '89, '90

Alsatian Tokay Pinot Gris Producers

Hugel
Domaine Weinbach†
Zind-Humbrecht
Josmeyer
Dopff 'Au Moulin'
Price Range $12–20
Preferred Vintages '88, '89

Easy-to-Find or Alternative Selection

Louis Jadot Mâcon-Villages
Price Range $10–14
Preferred Vintages '89, '90

CLAM CHOWDER MANHATTAN STYLE

The tomatoes and bacon of a savory Manhattan clam chowder call for a young Beaujolais, particularly those from the parishes of Fleurie or Brouilly. A Spanish red from the Rioja district goes nicely also.

French Beaujolais Producers

Georges Duboeuf Fleurie
Look for Domaine Bachelard
Chignard Fleurie†
Look for Les Moriers
Château de la Chaize Brouilly
Louis Jadot
Price Range $10–18
Preferred Vintages '89, '90

Spanish Red Rioja Producers

Berberana
Bodegas Olarra
La Rioja Alta
Marqués de Riscal
Marqués de Cáceres
Bodegas Bretón 'Loriñón'†
Price Range $8–15
Preferred Vintages '85, '87, '88 ('89 to cellar)

Easy-to-Find or Alternative Selection

Georges Duboeuf Beaujolais-Villages
Price Range $7–10
Preferred Vintages '89, '90

STEAMED CLAMS

The many ways to prepare steamed clams range from steamed clams in broth to steamed clams with roasted red peppers and onion. Be sure to choose a wine with firm acidity and no sweetness, such as a dry white Bordeaux, or a Sancerre or Pouilly-Fumé from France's Loire Valley. A well-made Washington Sauvignon Blanc is also tasty with most preparations for steamed clams.

French White Bordeaux Producers

Château Launey *Entre-Deux-Mers*
Château Bonnet *Entre-Deux-Mers*
Château La Louvière Blanc *Pessac Léognan*
Château Rahoul *Graves*†
Price Range $7–18
Preferred Vintages '88, '89, '90

French Sancerre Producers

Henri Bourgeois
Look for Côtes des Monts Damnés
Hippolyte Reverdy
Paul Cotat†
Look for La Grande Côte
Jean-Max Roger
Look for Chêne Marchand
Price Range $14–24
Preferred Vintages '89, '90

French Pouilly-Fumé Producers

J. M. Masson-Blondelet†
Look for Les Bascoins

Dagueneau†
Michel Redde
Pascal Jolivet
Price Range $14–20
Preferred Vintages '89, '90

Washington Sauvignon Blanc Producers

Barnard-Griffin *Washington State*†
Chateau Ste. Michelle *Columbia Valley*
Paul Thomas *Washington*†
Louis Facelli *Washington*†
Price Range $7–12
Preferred Vintages '89, '90

Easy-to-Find or Alternative Selection

Hogue Cellars Fumé Blanc *Washington State*
Price Range $7–10
Preferred Vintages '89, '90

ALASKAN KING CRAB

Alaskan king crab when served with drawn butter deserves one of the best white Burgundies or Chablis one can afford. The very rich meat is different in flavor from soft-shell or Dungeness crab, and French Chardonnay, from Chablis and the villages of Puligny and Chassagne, perfectly matches the flavor.

French White Burgundy Producers

PULIGNY-MONTRACHET
Étienne Sauzet†
Look for Les Combettes, Les Referts
Joseph Drouhin

Domaine Leflaive†
Look for Les Pucelles, Clavaillon
Chartron & Trébuchet
Henri Clerc

CHASSAGNE-MONTRACHET
Jean-Noël Gagnard†
Look for Les Caillerets
Michel Colin-Deléger†
Look for Les Vergers
Domaine Ramonet†
Look for Les Ruchottes
Michel Niellon†
Look for Les Vergers
Joseph Drouhin
Look for Marquis de Laguiche
Price Range $35–75
Preferred Vintages '88, '89
(Additionally, a white wine made from Pinot Noir grapes is produced in very limited quantities by Domaine Henri Gouges. The appellation is Nuits-St.-Georges and it carries the vineyard designation 'La Perrière.' Styled like a great white Burgundy, it is unique and well worth the effort to find. *Look for the '89 or '90 vintages.*)

French Chablis Producers

William Fèvre† (Also sold as Domaine Auffray)
Look for Montée de Tonnerre
René & Vincent Dauvissat
Look for Vaillons, La Forest, Les Clos
Louis Michel
Look for Montée de Tonnerre
Price Range $25–40
Preferred Vintages '88, '89

Value Recommendation

Joseph Drouhin Bourgogne Blanc 'Laforet'
Price Range $9–12
Preferred Vintages '89, '90

SOFT-SHELL CRAB

With soft-shell crab, I recommend a good dry white Bordeaux or a California Sauvignon Blanc.

French White Bordeaux Producers

Château Malartic-Lagravière *Pessac Léognan*
Château de Fieuzal *Pessac Léognan†*
Château La Louvière *Pessac Léognan*
Château Rahoul *Graves†*
Château Carbonnieux *Pessac Léognan*
Château de Rochemorin *Graves*
Price Range $15–35
Preferred Vintages '88, '89

California Sauvignon Blanc Producers

Babcock Vineyards *Santa Ynez Valley*
Robert Mondavi Winery *Napa Valley*
Ferrari-Carano *Sonoma County*
Price Range $7–12
Preferred Vintages '89, '90

Easy-to-Find or Alternative Selection

Kenwood Vineyards Sauvignon Blanc
    Sonoma County
Price Range $9–12
Preferred Vintages '89, '90

CRAB CAKES

A fruity, young Sauvignon Blanc from California or Washington is perfectly suited to the slightly spicy flavor of crab cakes.

California Sauvignon Blanc Producers

Grgich Hills Cellars *Napa Valley*
Matanzas Creek *Sonoma*
Robert Mondavi Winery *Napa Valley*
Duckhorn Vineyards *Napa Valley*†
Robert Pepi *Napa Valley*
Kenwood Vineyards *Sonoma County*
Silverado Vineyards *Napa Valley*
Price Range $8–15
Preferred Vintages '89, '90

Washington Sauvignon Blanc Producers

Hogue Cellars *Washington State*
Chinook *Yakima Valley*†
Barnard-Griffin *Washington State*†
Snoqualmie Winery *Washington*
Chateau Ste. Michelle *Columbia Valley*
Price Range $7–12
Preferred Vintages '89, '90

Easy-to-Find or Alternative Selection

Columbia Crest Sauvignon Blanc *Columbia Valley*
Price Range $6–9
Preferred Vintages '89, '90

DUNGENESS CRAB

The meat of fresh Dungeness crab is slightly sweet and requires a wine that is crisp and has bright fruit. Good, fresh California Sauvignon Blanc is a fine complement; however, I prefer a Washington dry white Riesling with crab. Also, German estate Riesling of

Kabinett quality is uniquely enjoyable, as the slightly sweet flavor nicely matches the richness of the meat.

California Sauvignon Blanc Producers

Chimney Rock *Napa Valley*†
Ferrari-Carano *Sonoma County*
Preston Vineyards & Winery *Dry Creek Valley*
Benziger *Sonoma*
Iron Horse Ranch & Vineyards *Sonoma*
Price Range $7–12
Preferred Vintages '89, '90

Washington Dry White Riesling Producers

Barnard-Griffin *Washington State*†
Chateau Ste. Michelle *Columbia Valley*
Louis Facelli *Washington*†
Hogue Cellars Reserve *Washington State*
Price Range $5–8
Preferred Vintages '88, '89, '90

German Riesling Kabinett Producers

Zilliken Saarburger Rausch *Saar*†
Fritz Haag Brauneberger Juffer-Sonnenuhr *Mosel*†
Egon Müller Scharzhöfberger *Saar*†
Von Hövel Oberemmeler Hütte *Saar*†
J. J. Prüm Wehlener Sonnenuhr *Mosel*†
Dr. Loosen Erdener Prälat *Mosel*†
Price Range $12–20
Preferred Vintages '83, '88, '89

Easy-to-Find or Alternative Selection

Beringer Vineyards Sauvignon Blanc *Napa Valley*
Price Range $7–10
Preferred Vintages '89, '90

CRAB STEAMED IN VERMOUTH

Crab that is steamed in its shell in a broth of butter, white wine, and vermouth requires a crisp white wine. I suggest a California Sauvignon Blanc or a French Pouilly-Fumé. An Alsatian Pinot Blanc also is pleasant with steamed crab.

California Sauvignon Blanc Producers

Grgich Hills Cellars *Napa Valley*
Matanzas Creek *Sonoma*
Robert Mondavi Winery *Napa Valley*
Duckhorn Vineyards *Napa Valley*†
Robert Pepi *Napa Valley*
Kenwood Vineyards *Sonoma County*
Silverado Vineyards *Napa Valley*
Price Range $8–15
Preferred Vintages '89, '90

French Pouilly-Fumé Producers

J. M. Masson-Blondelet†
Look for Les Bascoins
Paul Figeat
Ladoucette
Price Range $14–20
Preferred Vintages '89, '90

Alsatian Pinot Blanc Producers

Gustave Lorentz
Look for Réserve
Zind-Humbrecht

Muré
Hugel
Price Range $8–18
Preferred Vintages '88, '89

Easy-to-Find or Alternative Selection
F. E. Trimbach Pinot Blanc
Price Range $ 8–12
Preferred Vintages '88, '89

STEAMED OR BROILED LOBSTER

The rich flavor of the lobster meat combined with a butter sauce calls for big Chardonnays from California and great white Burgundies, particularly those from Grand Cru vineyards. French Champagne is also a wonderful and festive accompaniment to steamed or broiled lobster.

California Chardonnay Producers

Morgan Winery *Monterey*
Chalone Vineyards *Monterey*†
Grgich Hills Cellars *Napa Valley*
Fisher Vineyards *Sonoma*†
Look for Coach Insignia
Kistler Vineyards *Sonoma*†
Look for Dutton Ranch
Edna Valley Vineyard *Edna Valley*
Saintsbury *Carneros*
Acacia *Carneros*
Ferrari-Carano *Alexander Valley*†

Mount Eden Vineyards *Santa Cruz Mountains*†
Keenan Winery *Napa Valley*
Long Vineyards *Napa Valley*†
Price Range $15–30
Preferred Vintages '88, '89, '90

French Grand Cru White Burgundy Producers

BIENVENUES-BÂTARD-MONTRACHET OR BÂTARD-MONTRACHET
Étienne Sauzet†
Jean-Noël Gagnard†
Domaine Leflaive†

CHEVALIER-MONTRACHET
Domaine Leflaive†
Louis Jadot 'Les Demoiselles'†

LE MONTRACHET
Domaine Ramonet†
Joseph Drouhin 'Marquis de Laguiche'†
Remoissenet 'Baron Thénard'†
Price Range $75–200
Preferred Vintages '86, '88, '89

French Champagne Producers

Ayala Brut Aÿ†
Billecart Salmon 'Blanc de Blancs' *Mareuil-sur-Aÿ*†
A. Charbaut & Fils 'Blanc de Blancs' *Épernay*
Louis Roederer Brut Premier *Reims*
Philipponnat Brut *Mareuil-sur-Aÿ*
Taittinger Brut La Française *Reims*
Veuve Clicquot-Ponsardin Brut *Reims*
Price Range $25–40

Value Recommendations

Alderbrook Winery Chardonnay *Dry Creek Valley*
Zaca Mesa Chardonnay *Santa Barbara County*
Price Range $9–12
Preferred Vintages '89, '90

Clos du Val Chardonnay *Carneros*
Price Range $13–16
Preferred Vintages '89, '90

Joseph Drouhin Bourgogne Blanc 'Laforet'
Price Range $9–12
Preferred Vintages '89, '90

BAKED STUFFED LOBSTER

Rich and filling, this lobster preparation calls for a crisp yet full-bodied white wine to cleanse the palate. Great dry white Bordeaux, and white Burgundy from the commune of Chassagne are excellent. A California sparkling wine also goes well with baked stuffed lobster.

French White Bordeaux Producers

Château Laville Haut-Brion *Pessac Léognan*†
Château de Fieuzal *Pessac Léognan*†
Domaine de Chevalier Blanc *Pessac Léognan*†
Château Haut-Brion Blanc *Pessac Léognan*†
Price Range $40–100
Preferred Vintages '88, '89

French Chassagne-Montrachet Producers

Jean-Noël Gagnard
Look for Les Caillerets
Domaine Ramonet†
Look for Les Ruchottes
Michel Niellon†
Look for Les Vergers

Joseph Drouhin
Look for Marquis de Laguiche
Price Range $40–75
Preferred Vintages '86, '88, '89

California Sparkling Wine Producers

Roederer Estate Brut *Anderson Valley*
Domaine Carneros Brut *Carneros*
Mumm Cuvée Napa Brut Prestige *Napa Valley*
Look for Winery Lake Reserve
Piper-Sonoma Brut *Sonoma*
Gloria Ferrer Brut *Sonoma*
Look for Carneros Cuvée
Schramsberg Blanc de Blancs *Napa Valley*
Maison Deutz Brut *Santa Barbara*
Michel Tribaut Brut *Monterey*
Price Range $13–25

Value Recommendation

Château de Cruzeau Blanc *Graves*
Price Range $10–12
Preferred Vintages '88, '89

Easy-to-Find or Alternative Selection

Domaine Chandon Brut *Napa Valley*
Price Range $9–15

LOBSTER
NEWBURG

The cream, egg, and Madeira in this
classic preparation give it a thick, rich
taste. I love to have good French
Chablis and intense Rhône Valley whites

with lobster Newburg. However, white Burgundy or California Chardonnays with good acidity also complement this meal.

French Chablis Producers

William Fèvre (Also sold as Domaine Auffray)
Look for Montée de Tonnerre
René & Vincent Dauvissat
Look for Vaillons, La Forest, Les Clos, Les Preuses
François Raveneau†
Look for Chapelot, Montée de Tonnerre, Clos, Butteaux
Louis Michel
Look for Montée de Tonnerre
Price Range $25–45
Preferred Vintages '88, '89

French White Rhône Valley Producers

Château de Beaucastel Châteauneuf-du-Pape Blanc
Look for Roussanne 'Vieille Vigne'†
E. Guigal Condrieu†
Georges Vernay Condrieu†
Château du Rozay Condrieu†
Look for Coteaux de Vernon
J. L. Chave Hermitage Blanc†
Price Range $25–50
Preferred Vintages '88, '89
(Additionally, the rare and limited Château-Grillet, which is its own appellation in the northern part of the Rhône Valley, is made from Viognier grapes and is well worth seeking out. *Look for the '88 and '89 vintages.* From California, Viognier has been bottled in small quantities by La Jota Vineyard and Joseph Phelps Vineyards. The Joseph Phelps Vineyards Viognier bears the 'Vin du Mistral' label. *Look for the '90 vintage.*)

French White Burgundy Producers

PULIGNY-MONTRACHET

Étienne Sauzet†
Look for Les Referts, Les Combettes
Joseph Drouhin
Domaine Leflaive†
Look for Les Pucelles, Clavaillon
Chartron & Trébuchet
Henri Clerc
Price Range $35–50
Preferred Vintages '88, '89

California Chardonnay Producers

Shafer Vineyards *Napa Valley*
Smith-Madrone *Napa Valley*†
The Gainey Vineyard *Santa Barbara County*†
Chateau Montelena *Napa Valley*
Clos du Val *Carneros*
Price Range $13–20
Preferred Vintages '88, '89, '90

Value Recommendations

Domaine Talmard Mâcon-Chardonnay
Price Range $10–14
Preferred Vintages '89, '90

St. Andrews Winery Chardonnay *Napa Valley*
Price Range $9–12
Preferred Vintages '89, '90

Easy-to-Find or Alternative Selection

Kendall Jackson Chardonnay 'Vintner's
  Reserve' *California*
Price Range $10–14
Preferred Vintages '89, '90

MUSSELS STEAMED IN WINE AND BUTTER

A wide range of dry white wines match the flavor of steamed mussels. When the preparation calls for drawn butter, try a California Chardonnay from Sonoma County. If there is garlic and herbs in the preparation, I suggest a California Sauvignon Blanc or an Italian Verdicchio.

California Chardonnay Producers

Dehlinger Winery *Sonoma*†
Murphy-Goode *Alexander Valley*
B. R. Cohn *Sonoma*†
Kistler Vineyards *Sonoma*†
Look for Dutton Ranch
Matanzas Creek *Sonoma*
Sonoma-Cutrer *Sonoma*†
Look for Les Pierres
Price Range $12–25
Preferred Vintages '88, '89, '90

California Sauvignon Blanc Producers

Duckhorn Vineyards *Napa Valley*†
Caymus Vineyards *Napa Valley*
Frog's Leap Wine Cellars *Napa Valley*
Ferrari-Carano *Sonoma County*
Spottswoode Vineyard & Winery *Napa Valley*†
Price Range $10–15
Preferred Vintages '88, '89, '90

Italian Verdicchio Producers

Colonnara 'Cuprese'
Garafoli†
Look for Macrina
Fazi-Battaglia
Umani Ronchi
Look for Casal di Sera
Price Range $7–14
Preferred Vintages (*youngest available*)

Easy-to-Find or Alternative Selection

Kenwood Vineyards Chardonnay *Sonoma*
Price Range $12–15
Preferred Vintages '89, '90

STEAMED MUSSELS WITH TOMATO AND SAFFRON

The flavor of tomatoes and saffron add a new dimension to steamed mussels. Just as with mussels steamed in wine and butter, many white wines go very nicely with this meal. But lighter-bodied reds can also be served, and they match the tomato and saffron beautifully. Try an Italian Valpolicella or a French Côtes du Roussillon red.

Italian Valpolicella Producers

Masi
Look for Serègo Alighieri

Le Ragose
Allegrini
Zonin
Price Range $7–15
Preferred Vintages '88, '90

French Côtes du Roussillon Producers

Caramany†
La Tour de France†
Château Cap de Fouste†
Domaine de Canterrane†
Château de Jau†
Price Range $8–13
Preferred Vintages '88, '89

Easy-to-Find or Alternative Selection

Masi Valpolicella
Price Range $7–10
Preferred Vintages '88, '90

OYSTERS ON THE HALF SHELL

The succulent, pungent flavor of fresh oysters is a perfect marriage with the crisp and flinty taste of French Chablis. The two combine to create an intense gustatory experience. French Champagne tastes great with oysters and is a refreshing, albeit expensive, alternative.

French Chablis Producers

Louis Michel Chablis
René & Vincent Dauvissat Chablis 1er Cru
Look for Vaillons, La Forest

William Fèvre Chablis 1er Cru (Also sold as
    Domaine Auffray)
Look for Montée de Tonnerre
François Raveneau Chablis Grand Cru†
Look for Clos, Valmur, Blanchot
Price Range $15–60
Preferred Vintages '88, '89

French Champagne Producers

Ayala Brut *Aÿ*†
Billecart Salmon 'Blanc de Blancs' *Mareuil-
    sur-Aÿ*†
Charbaut & Fils 'Blanc de Blancs' *Épernay*
Drappier Carte d'Or' Brut *Urville*†
Louis Roederer Brut Premier *Reims*
Philipponnat Brut *Mareuil-sur-Aÿ*
Taittinger Brut La Française *Reims*
Veuve Clicquot-Ponsardin Brut *Reims*
Price Range $25–40

Value Recommendation

Joseph Drouhin Bourgogne Blanc 'Laforet'
Price Range $9–12
Preferred Vintages '89, 90

Easy-to-Find or Alternative Selection

Domaine Chandon Brut *Napa Valley*
Price Range $9–15

BAKED OYSTERS

The type of stuffing or topping to be
used will determine the style of the
wine. If the preparation is hot or spicy,
try a dry Sauvignon Blanc from
California with plenty of body. For
preparations such as oysters Florentine,

made with spinach, or oysters with lemon and capers, select a drier, lighter Sauvignon Blanc from Washington or a <u>Muscadet from France.</u>

California Sauvignon Blanc Producers

Matanzas Creek *Sonoma*
Robert Mondavi Winery *Napa Valley*
Look for Reserve
Grgich Hills Cellars *Napa Valley*
Buena Vista *Lake County*
Price Range $8–15
Preferred Vintages '89, '90

Washington Sauvignon Blanc Producers

Snoqualmie Winery *Washington*
Barnard-Griffin *Washington State*†
Arbor Crest *Columbia Valley*†
Paul Thomas *Washington*†
Chateau Ste. Michelle *Columbia Valley*
Price Range $7–12
Preferred Vintages '89, '90

French Muscadet Producers

Louis Métaireau
Look for Cuvée One†
Château de la Noë
Château Ragotière
Marcel Martin
Marquis de Goulaine
Price Range $8–15
Preferred Vintages '89, '90

Easy-to-Find or Alternative Selection

Hogue Cellars Fumé Blanc *Washington State*
Price Range $7–10
Preferred Vintages '89, '90

OYSTER STEW

The rich flavor of the cream and butter and the spice of the pepper make oyster stew different from other oyster dishes. A full-bodied, young California or Oregon Chardonnay or a richly flavored California Semillon is great. The style of Alsatian Riesling, dry and full, is perfect.

California Chardonnay Producers

Chateau St. Jean *Sonoma County*
Crichton Hall *Napa Valley*
Folie-à-Deux *Napa Valley*
Smith-Madrone *Napa Valley*†
Saint Andrews Winery *Napa Valley*
DeLoach Vineyards *Sonoma County*
Price Range $12–18
Preferred Vintages '88, '89, '90

Oregon Chardonnay Producers

Tualatin Vineyards *Willamette Valley*
Look for Reserve
The Eyrie Vineyards *Willamette Valley*
Argyle *Oregon*†
Rex Hill Vineyards *Willamette Valley*†
Adelsheim Vineyard *Willamette Valley*†
Bethel Heights Vineyard *Willamette Valley*
Price Range $13–20
Preferred Vintages '88, '89

California Semillon Producers

Duckhorn Vineyards 'Decoy' *Napa Valley*†
Alderbrook Winery *Dry Creek Valley*
Benziger *Sonoma*
Price Range $7–12
Preferred Vintages '88, '89, '90

Alsatian Riesling Producers

Domaine Weinbach†
F. E. Trimbach
Zind-Humbrecht
Look for Réserve†
Hugel
Ostertag †
Look for Muenchberg
Price Range $9–20
Preferred Vintages '88, '89

Easy-to-Find or Alternative Selection

Fetzer Vineyards Chardonnay 'Barrel Select'
  Mendocino
Price Range $9–12
Preferred Vintages '89, '90

PAN-FRIED
OYSTERS

Lightly battered oysters sautéed in
butter are complemented by a wide
range of domestic Sauvignon Blancs
and by the rich, yet crisp style of French
Sancerre. Also, a fresh, young dry white
Bordeaux or the smoky style of Pouilly-
Fumé matches these flavors well.

California Sauvignon Blanc Producers

Caymus Vineyards *Napa Valley*
Ferrari-Carano *Sonoma County*
Benziger *Sonoma*
Iron Horse Ranch & Vineyards *Sonoma*
Price Range $7–12
Preferred Vintages '89, '90

French Sancerre Producers

Henri Bourgeois
Look for Côtes des Monts Damnés†
Jean-Max Roger
Paul Cotat†
Alphonse Mellot
Hippolyte Reverdy
Look for Les Perriers
Price Range $14–20
Preferred Vintages '89, '90

French White Bordeaux Producers

Château La Louvière Blanc *Pessac Léognan*
Château Launay *Entre-Deux-Mers*
Château Fieuzal Blanc *Pessac Léognan*†
Château Bonnet *Entre-Deux-Mers*
Price Range $7–18
Preferred Vintages '88, '89, '90

French Pouilly-Fumé Producers

J. M. Masson-Blondelet†
Look for Les Bascoins
Paul Figeat
Ladoucette
Price Range $14–20
Preferred Vintages '89, '90

Easy-to-Find or Alternative Selection

Beringer Vineyards Sauvignon Blanc *Napa
Valley*
Price Range $7–10
Preferred Vintages '89, '90

COQUILLES ST.
JACQUES

The rich flavor of scallops, cream, and
cheese calls for a big white wine with

good acidity and body. A French Chablis from one of the premier cru vineyards is my first choice. An Italian Vernaccia di San Gimignano or an Oregon Pinot Gris also marries well with these flavors.

French Chablis Producers

René & Vincent Dauvissat
Look for Vaillons
Louis Michel
Look for Montée de Tonnerre
William Fèvre (Also sold as Domaine Auffray)
Look for Montée de Tonnerre
François Raveneau†
Look for Chapelot
Price Range $18–35
Preferred Vintages '88, '89

Italian Vernaccia Producers

Teruzzi & Puthod
Look for Terre di Tufo†
Falchini
San Quirico
Giannina
Price Range $7–18
Preferred Vintages '89, '90

Oregon Pinot Gris Producers

The Eyrie Vineyards *Willamette Valley*
Adelsheim Vineyards *Oregon†*
Ponzi Vineyards *Oregon†*
Rex Hill Vineyards *Oregon†*
Price Range $9–14
Preferred Vintages '89, '90

Easy-to-Find or Alternative Selection

Joseph Drouhin Chablis
Price Range $14–18
Preferred Vintages '89, '90

SCALLOPS STEAMED IN WINE AND BUTTER

The flavor of scallops steamed in wine and butter requires a delicate, complex, dry white wine. I recommend an Italian Pinot Grigio or a French Savennières.

Italian Pinot Grigio Producers

Gianni Vescovo
Borgo Conventi†
Livio Felluga
Price Range $10–17
Preferred Vintages '89, '90

French Savennières Producers

Domaine des Baumard†
Look for Clos du Papillon
Château d'Epiré
Domaine du Closel†
Château de la Roche-aux-Moines†
Price Range $12–20
Preferred Vintages '88, '89

Easy-to-Find or Alternative Selection

Santa Margherita Pinot Grigio
Price Range $14–17
Preferred Vintages '89, '90

GRILLED PRAWNS OR SCAMPI

Buttery, oaky, full-bodied California Chardonnays and lush, rich, complex Meursaults are perfect with grilled prawns or scampi. Australian Chardonnay provides a nice alternative.

California Chardonnay Producers

Kistler Vineyards *Sonoma*†
Look for Dutton Ranch
Hess Collection *Napa Valley*
Crichton Hall *Napa Valley*
Babcock Vineyards *Santa Ynez Valley*
Burgess Cellars *Napa Valley*
Grgich Hills Cellars *Napa Valley*
Au Bon Climat *Santa Barbara*†
Price Range $13–25
Preferred Vintages '88, '89, '90

French Meursault Producers

François Jobard†
Look for Meursault-Charmes
Comte Lafon†
Look for Meursault-Genevrières
René Manuel
Domaine Darnat†
Joseph Drouhin
Look for Meursault-Perrières
Domaine Matrot
Price Range $30–45
Preferred Vintages '88, '89

Australian Chardonnay Producers

Mountadam *Eden Valley*†
Lindeman's *Padthaway*

Rothbury Estate *Hunter Valley*
Look for Brokenback Vineyard
Wyndham Estate *Southeastern Australia*
Cassegrain *Southeastern Australia*†
Look for Fromenteau Vineyard
Montrose *Mudgee*†
Price Range $12–24
Preferred Vintages '87, '89, '90

Value Recommendations

J. Pedroncelli Chardonnay *Sonoma County*
Zaca Mesa Chardonnay *Santa Barbara County*
Price Range $9–12
Preferred Vintages '89, '90

Easy-to-Find or Alternative Selection

Lindeman's Chardonnay 'Bin 65' *South-eastern Australia*
Price Range $6–9
Preferred Vintage '90

CURRIED SHRIMP

Curried shrimp is difficult to match with wine. The flavors of turmeric and pepper in a moderately spiced shrimp curry marry well with Alsatian and Oregon Gewürztraminers.

Alsatian Gewürztraminer Producers

Zind-Humbrecht
Hugel
Marcel Diess†
Muré†
Look for Clos St. Landelin
Price Range $12–20
Preferred Vintages '88, '89

Oregon Gewürztraminer Producers

Tualatin Vineyards *Willamette Valley*
Elk Cove Vineyards *Willamette Valley*
Amity Vineyards *Oregon*†
Bridgeview Vineyards *Oregon*†
Price Range $7–12
Preferred Vintages *'88, '89, '90*

Easy-to-Find or Alternative Selection

F. E. Trimbach Gewürztraminer *Alsace*
Price Range $9–12
Preferred Vintages *'88, '89*

SHRIMP IN DILL
CREAM SAUCE

The flavor of dill weed narrows the
normal range of white wines that go
with shrimp. Both dry white Bordeaux
and California Sauvignon Blanc are
tasty choices.

French White Bordeaux Producers

Château de Launay *Entre-Deux-Mers*
Château de Fieuzal *Pessac Léognan*†
Château Carbonnieux Blanc *Pessac Léognan*
Château Couhins-Lurton *Pessac Léognan*
Château La Louvière *Pessac Léognan*
Château Malartic-Lagravière *Pessac Léognan*
Price Range $13–30
Preferred Vintages *'88, '89*

California Sauvignon Blanc Producers

Robert Pepi *Napa Valley*
Grgich Hills Cellars *Napa Valley*

Frog's Leap Wine Cellars *Napa Valley*
Silverado Vineyards *Napa Valley*
Kenwood Vineyards *Sonoma County*
Preston Vineyards & Winery *Dry Creek Valley*
Beaulieu Vineyards Fumé Blanc *California*
Price Range $8–15
***Preferred Vintages** '89, '90*

Easy-to-Find or Alternative Selection

Hogue Cellars Fumé Blanc *Washington State*
Price Range $7–10
***Preferred Vintages** '89, '90*

SHRIMP WITH SAFFRON RICE

The subtle complexity of saffron and the delicate flavor of shrimp require a well-balanced dry white wine. Choose a white Burgundy from a less well known commune such as Savigny-les-Beaune, Pernand-Vergelesses or Saint-Aubin. Also tasty are the better Oregon Chardonnays, which tend to have more acidity than their California counterparts.

French Savigny-les-Beaune Blanc Producers

Chartron & Trébuchet
Bitouzet†
Louis Jadot
Pierre Guillemot†
Price Range $15–25
Preferred Vintages '88, '89

French Pernand-Vergelesses Blanc Producers

Tollot-Voarick†
Antonin Guyon
Chanson Père & Fils
Remoissenet 'Baron Thénard'†
Look for Ile des Vergelesses
Price Range $15–25
Preferred Vintages '88, '89

French Saint-Aubin Blanc Producers

Gérard Thomas†
Maison Clerget†
Domaine Roux Père & Fils†
Price Range $15–25
Preferred Vintages '88, '89

Oregon Chardonnay Producers

Tualatin Vineyards *Willamette Valley*
Look for Reserve
The Eyrie Vineyards *Willamette Valley*
Argyle *Oregon*†
Cameron Winery *Willamette Valley*†
Look for Abbey Ridge Reserve
Adelsheim Vineyard *Willamette Valley*†
Bethel Heights Vineyard *Willamette Valley*†
Price Range $13–20
Preferred Vintages '88, '89

Value Recommendation

Knudsen Erath Winery Chardonnay *Oregon*
Price Range $9–12
Preferred Vintages '89, '90

Easy-to-Find or Alternative Selection

Louis Jadot Mâcon-Villages
Price Range $10–14
Preferred Vintages '89, '90

PASTA DISHES

The variety of pasta seems endless and the number of different wines that can be served is vast. Tradition suggests that the wine be Italian, as good whites and reds from Italy all seem to go well with pasta. Look to the sauce for the specific wine selection.

CANNELLONI

Recipes for cannelloni vary, but the traditional style has a filling of chicken, liver, and prosciutto with Parmesan cheese. These ingredients are complemented by either white or red wines, but both should be reasonably full bodied and have excellent fruit. Try an Italian Chardonnay, or a Dolcetto from the Piedmont region. If a sauce other than white sauce is used on the cannelloni, see the section on individual pasta sauces (page 179).

Italian Chardonnay Producers

Bollini
Tenuta Villanova
Tiefenbrunner
Borgo Conventi†
Maculan†
Berutti Pietro 'La Spinona'†
Price Range $10–25
Preferred Vintages '88, '89, '90

Italian Dolcetto Producers

Chionetti†
Look for San Luigi, La Costa, Briccolero
Cavallotto
Aldo Conterno
Ceretto
Clerico†
Berutti Pietro 'La Spinona'†
Bruno Giacosa
Price Range $12–20
Preferred Vintages '88, '89

Easy-to-Find or Alternative Selection

Franco Fiorina Dolcetto d'Alba
Price Range $9–12
Preferred Vintages '88, '89

LASAGNE

Layered with cheese and sauce, lasagne calls for rich, medium- to full-bodied red wines from Tuscany. Many of the new Sangiovese-Cabernet blends, labeled as Vino da Tavola, are great with lasagne, but bigger style Chianti Classico also goes nicely.

Italian Red Vino da Tavola Producers

Frescobaldi 'Pomino Rosso'
Fattoria di Felsina 'Fontalloro'†
L. Antinori 'Ornellaia'†
Castello di Rampolla 'Sammarco'†
Fontodi 'Flaccianello'†
Ruffino 'Cabreo'
Price Range $15–30
Preferred Vintages '85, '86, '88

Italian Chianti Classico Producers

Fontodi
Fattoria di Felsina
Castello di Fonterutoli
Castello di Cacchiano†
Look for Riserva
Castello di Rampolla†
Price Range $8–15
Preferred Vintages '87, '88, '89

Easy-to-Find or Alternative Selection

Frescobaldi Chianti Classico
Price Range $5–8
Preferred Vintages '89, '90

MANICOTTI

Filled with mozzarella, mushrooms, veal, and garlic, and topped with tomato sauce, manicotti calls for medium- to full-bodied Italian reds. Try a Montepulciano d'Abruzzo or a Barbera d'Alba.

Italian Montepulciano d'Abruzzo Producers

Barone Cornacchia
Casal Thaulero
Rosso della Quercia
Valentini†
Cantalupo
Price Range $7–25
Preferred Vintages '85, '86, '88

Italian Barbera d'Alba Producers

Coppo
Look for Camp du Rouss†

Berutti Pietro 'La Spinona'
Montanello†
Giacomo Ascheri
Ceretto
Luigi Einaudi
Cogno-Marcarini†
Bruno Giacosa
Giuseppe Rinaldi
Price Range $7–18
Preferred Vintages '88, '89

Easy-to-Find or Alternative Selection
Ruffino Chianti Classico
Price Range $5–8
Preferred Vintages '88, '89

RAVIOLI

Whether filled with cheese or meat, ravioli has a thick texture. Be sure the wine has plenty of acidity to cut through the weight and cleanse the palate. For butter and cream sauce preparations, I recommend a bottle of Pinot Grigio or Chardonnay from northern Italy. With marinara sauce, a good complement is a bottle of the new blends of Sangiovese and Cabernet Sauvignon aged in oak barrels and simply classified as red Vino da Tavola. A young Dolcetto d'Alba is also a nice match.

Italian Pinot Grigio Producers
Gianni Vescovo
Plozner

Santa Margherita
Tiefenbrunner
Herrnhofer†
Price Range $10–17
Preferred Vintages '89, '90

Italian Chardonnay Producers

Bollini
Tenuta Villanova
Tiefenbrunner
Borgo Conventi†
Maculan
Berutti Pietro 'La Spinona'†
Price Range $10–25
Preferred Vintages '88, '89

Italian Red Vino da Tavola Producers

Frescobaldi 'Pomino Rosso'
Fattoria di Felsina 'Fontalloro'†
Fontodi 'Flaccianello'†
L. Antinori 'Ornellaia'†
Castello dei Rampolla 'Sammarco'†
Ruffino 'Cabreo'
Antinori 'Tignanello'†
Price Range $15–30
Preferred Vintages '83, '85, '86, '88

Italian Dolcetto d'Alba Producers

Cavallotto
Aldo Conterno
Ceretto
Clerico†
Fenocchio
Berutti Pietro 'La Spinona'†
Bruno Giacosa
Franco Fiorina
Price Range $12–20
Preferred Vintages '89, '90
**(Luciano di Giacomi produces a wine called
Bricco del Drago, which is a marvelous blend of
Dolcetto and Nebbiolo grapes from vineyards
near Alba. Look for the Vigna 'd la Mace Riserva.)**

Value Recommendation

Antinori Chianti Classico
Price Range $9–12
Preferred Vintages '88, '89

Easy-to-Find or Alternative Selection

Antinori 'Santa Christina'
Price Range $5–8
Preferred Vintages '88, '89

SPAGHETTI WITH MEAT SAUCE

A straw-covered flask of cheap Chianti immediately comes to mind. But there are many different reds from Italy that go well with this classic. Try a Montepulciano d'Abruzzo from the Abruzzi district in Italy. The heavier Chianti Rufina from around Firenze, and fruity, young Dolcetto d'Alba are also recommended.

Italian Montepulciano d'Abruzzo Producers

Barone Cornacchia
Casal Thaulero
Rosso della Quercia
Price Range $8–12
Preferred Vintages '88, '89

Italian Chianti Rufina Producers

Selvapiana
Fattoria di Bossi†

Travignoli†
Frescobaldi 'Castello di Nipozzano'
Price Range $12–15
Preferred Vintages '87, '88, '89

Italian Dolcetto d'Alba Producers

Cavallotto
Clerico†
Fenocchio
Berutti Pietro 'La Spinona'†
Bruno Giacosa
Franco Fiorina
Price Range $12–20
Preferred Vintages '88, '89

Easy-to-Find or Alternative Selections

Antinori Chianti Classico
Price Range $9–12
Preferred Vintages '88, '89

Frescobaldi Chianti Classico
Price Range $5–8
Preferred Vintages '89, '90

PASTA SAUCES
ALFREDO SAUCE

The butter, cream, and Parmesan cheese used in making Alfredo sauce are the flavors to match. Good whites such as Pinot Bianco from northern Italy and Vernaccia di San Gimignano from Tuscany are well suited to this dish.

Italian Pinot Bianco Producers

Enofriulia
Gianni Vescovo

Plozner
Morasutti
Tiefenbrunner
Herrnhofer†
Price Range $7–15
***Preferred Vintages** '89, '90*

Italian Vernaccia Producers

Teruzzi & Puthod
Look for Terre di Tufo†
Falchini
San Quirico
Giannina
Price Range $7–18
***Preferred Vintages** '89, '90*

Easy-to-Find or Alternative Selection

Santa Margherita Pinot Grigio
Price Range $14–17
***Preferred Vintages** '89, '90*

CARBONARA SAUCE

Whether it is made with true Italian bacon (pancetta), prosciutto, or American bacon, carbonara sauce is creamy and slightly smoky in nature. Drier Italian whites such as Orvieto Classico and Pinot Bianco are perfect, although Italian Chianti Classico goes very nicely too.

Italian Orvieto Classico Producers

Barbi
Barberani
Bigi†
Look for Vigneto Torricella
Decugnano dei Barbi†

Antinori
Price Range $7–12
Preferred Vintages ’89, ’90

Italian Pinot Bianco Producers

Enofriulia
Gianni Vescovo
Plozner
Morasutti
Tiefenbrunner
Hermhofer†
Price Range $7–15
Preferred Vintages ’89, ’90

Italian Chianti Classico Producers

San Giusto a Rentennano †
Castelgreve
Gabbiano
Castello di Ama
Look for San Lorenzo
Isole e Olena
Castello di Querceto
San Felice
Price Range $8–15
Preferred Vintages ’87, ’88, ’89

Easy-to-Find or Alternative Selection

Ruffino Orvieto Classico
Price Range $7–10
Preferred Vintages ’89, ’90

CHEESE SAUCE

Three or four cheeses are usually combined in this kind of sauce. The fruity style of fresh Pinot Grigio matches the different cheeses exceptionally well. Yet the thick texture of the cheeses also allows for bolder, moderately tannic reds. Try a Chianti Rufina or a fruity Dolcetto d'Alba.

Italian Pinot Grigio Producers

Tiefenbrunner
Santa Margherita
Borgo Conventi†
Gianni Vescovo
Price Range $10–17
Preferred Vintages '89, '90

Italian Chianti Rufina Producers

Selvapiana
Fattoria di Bossi†
Frescobaldi 'Castello di Nipozzano'
Price Range $12–15
Preferred Vintages '87, '88, '89

Italian Dolcetto d'Alba Producers

Cavallotto
Aldo Conterno
Ceretto
Clerico†
Berutti Pietro 'La Spinona'†
Bruno Giacosa
Price Range $12–20
Preferred Vintages '88, '89

Easy-to-Find or Alternative Selection

Frescobaldi Chianti Classico
Price Range $5–8
Preferred Vintages '89, '90

CLAM SAUCE

White clam sauce, dominated by the flavors of garlic and clams, calls for crisp, spicy white wines such as an Italian Gavi or Arneis from the Piedmont. Good Soave Classico with its almost salty flavor is also a nice complement. For red clam sauce recommendations see Seafood (di Mare) Sauce (page 184).

Italian Gavi Producers

Fausto Gemme 'La Merlina'
La Scolca 'Gavi dei Gavi'
La Battistina
Granduca
Price Range $12–20
Preferred Vintages '89, '90

Italian Arneis Producers

Ceretto 'Blangé'†
Bruno Giacosa†
Castello di Neive†
Price Range $12–20
Preferred Vintages '89, '90

Italian Soave Classico Producers

Anselmi
Look for Capitel Foscarino
Boscaini
Masi
Look for Col Baraca
Pieropan
Look for La Rocca
Price Range $8–15
Preferred Vintages '89, '90

Easy-to-Find or Alternative Selection

Masi Soave Classico
Price Range $7–10
Preferred Vintages '89, '90

SEAFOOD (DI MARE) SAUCE

The addition of shellfish and seafood to tomato sauce creates salsa di mare. Whites and reds both work nicely with this sauce. If choosing a white wine, try a Vernaccia di San Gimignano or a fruity Pinot Grigio. Valpolicella would be a nice red.

Italian Vernaccia Producers

Teruzzi & Puthod
Look for Terre di Tufo†
Falchini
San Quirico
Giannina
Price Range $7–18
Preferred Vintages '89, '90

Italian Pinot Grigio Producers

Tiefenbrunner
Santa Margherita
Borgo Conventi†
Gianni Vescovo
Price Range $10–17
Preferred Vintages '89, '90

Italian Valpolicella Producers

Masi
Look for Serègo Alighieri
Le Ragose
Allegrini
Zonin
Price Range $7–15
Preferred Vintages '89, '90

Masi Valpolicella
Price Range $7–10
***Preferred Vintages** '89, '90*

MARINARA SAUCE

Rich with tomatoes, onion, garlic, basil, and anchovies, marinara sauce is complemented by the crisp, dry flavors of Orvieto Classico. Young Italian Chianti with big fruit is also a classic companion to marinara sauce.

Italian Orvieto Classico Producers

Barbi
Barberani
Bigi†
Look for Vigneto Torricella
Decugnano dei Barbi†
Antinori
Ruffino
Price Range $7–12
***Preferred Vintages** '89, '90*

Italian Chianti Producers

Castelgreve
Gabbiano
Isole e Olena
Castello di Querceto
San Felice
Price Range $8–15
***Preferred Vintages** '87, '88, '89*

Easy-to-Find or Alternative Selection

Ruffino Orvieto Classico
Price Range $7–10
***Preferred Vintages** '89, '90*

PESTO SAUCE

Garlic, pine nuts, and fresh basil give pesto sauce an intense, almost sweet flavor. Either a crisp young Vernaccia di San Gimignano or a Verdicchio from a great producer is a wonderful companion to pesto sauce.

Italian Vernaccia Producers

Teruzzi & Puthod
Look for Terre di Tufo†
Falchini
San Quirico
Giannina
Price Range $7–18
Preferred Vintages '89, '90

Italian Verdicchio Producers

Colonnara 'Cuprese'
Garafoli†
Look for Macrina
Fazi-Battaglia
Umani Ronchi
Look for Casal di Sera
Price Range $7–14
Preferred Vintages (youngest available)

Easy-to-Find or Alternative Selection

Ruffino Orvieto Classico
Price Range $7–10
Preferred Vintages '89, '90

PUTTANESCA SAUCE

The zestiness of capers, olives, anchovies, garlic, and plum tomatoes makes puttanesca a sauce for those who like intense flavors. Earthy Italian whites such as Vernaccia di San Gimignano or Italian red Vino da Tavola blends match the bold taste.

Italian Vernaccia Producers

Teruzzi & Puthod
Look for Terre di Tufo†
Falchini
San Quirico
Price Range $7–18
Preferred Vintages '89 '90

Italian Red Vino da Tavola Producers

Frescobaldi 'Pomino Rosso'
Fattoria di Felsina 'Fontalloro'†
L. Antinori 'Ornellaia'†
Castello di Rampolla 'Sammarco'†
Fontodi 'Flaccianello'†
Ruffino 'Cabreo'
Antinori 'Tignanello'†
Price Range $15–35 +
Preferred Vintages '85, '86, '88

Easy-to-Find or Alternative Selection

Ruffino Chianti Classico
Price Range $5–8
Preferred Vintages '88, '89

TOMATO SAUCE

Contrary to what you might expect, red wines aren't mandatory with tomato sauce. Many dry white wines, such as Italian Pinot Grigio, complement the flavor of tomato, basil, oregano, and onion. If you prefer a red wine, I would suggest a spicy, lighter style Italian red such as Chianti or Barbera.

Italian Pinot Grigio Producers

Livio Felluga
Gianni Vescovo
Gradnik
Jermann†
Enofriulia
Borgo Conventi†
Price Range $10–17
Preferred Vintages '89, '90

Italian Chianti Producers

San Giusto a Rentennano†
Castelgreve
Gabbiano
Isole e Olena
Castello di Querceto
San Felice
Price Range $8–15
Preferred Vintages '87, '88, '89

Italian Barbera d'Alba Producers

Berutti Pietro 'La Spinona'
Montanello†
Cogno-Marcarini†
Ceretto
Luigi Einaudi
Bruno Giacosa
Giuseppe Rinaldi
Price Range $7–18
Preferred Vintages '88 '89

Easy-to-Find or Alternative Selection

Santa Margherita Pinot Grigio
Price Range $14–17
Preferred Vintages '89, '90

RICE DISHES

Rice dishes are becoming increasingly popular main courses. Consider individual combinations of spices and flavors when selecting wines to match these preparations.

CURRIED RICE

The degree of spice in a curry varies from light to intense. When the preparation is light to medium, try a moderately priced white Bordeaux or a California Sauvignon Blanc. A French Bandol rosé also stands up to moderate spice. If the spice is intense, try an Oregon Gewürztraminer to freshen the palate.

French White Bordeaux Producers

Château Bonnet *Entre-Deux-Mers*
Château de Launay *Entre-Deux-Mers*
Château Raspide *Langon*
Château Ferrande *Castres*
Price Range $7–13
Preferred Vintages '88, '89, '90

California Sauvignon Blanc Producers

Sterling Vineyards *Napa Valley*
Beringer Vineyards *Napa Valley*
Ferrari-Carano *Sonoma County*
Hanna Winery *Sonoma*†
Price Range $7–12
Preferred Vintages '89, '90

French Bandol Rosé Producers

Moulin des Costes†
Domaine Tempier†
Château Vannières†
Domaine de L'Hermitage†
Price Range $12–18
Preferred Vintages '89, '90

Oregon Gewürztraminer Producers

Tualatin Vineyards *Willamette Valley*
Elk Cove Vineyards *Willamette Valley*
Amity Vineyards *Oregon*†
Bridgeview Vineyards *Oregon*†
Price Range $7–12
Preferred Vintages '88, '89, '90

Easy-to-Find or Alternative Selections

Beaulieu Vineyards Fumé Blanc *Napa Valley*
Price Range $6–9
Preferred Vintages '89, '90

Kenwood Vineyards Sauvignon Blanc
  Sonoma County
Price Range $9–12
Preferred Vintages '89, '90

JAMBALAYA

The complex flavor of jambalaya is a blend of ham, chicken, pork sausage, chili powder, green pepper, onion, and garlic. A full-flavored California Zinfandel, Petite Sirah or Syrah will stand up to these ingredients. Some versions call for seafood instead of the chicken. With this preparation, a good California Dry Chenin Blanc is an excellent match.

California Zinfandel Producers

Rafanelli Winery *Sonoma*†
Gundlach Bundschu *Sonoma*†
Fetzer Vineyards 'Barrel Select' *North Coast*
Ridge 'Geyserville' *Sonoma*
Price Range $7–13
Preferred Vintages '87, '88, '89

California Petite Sirah / Syrah Producers

Joseph Phelps Vineyards *Napa Valley*
McDowell Valley Vineyards *McDowell Valley*
Look for Les Vieux Cépages
Guenoc Winery *Lake County*
Ridge 'York Creek' *Sonoma*
Price Range $8–15
Preferred Vintages '85, '87, '88
**(Edmunds St. John in Berkeley produces a
nonvintage American red table wine called 'Les
Côtes Sauvage' from a blend of California Syrah
and Washington Grenache. Bonny Doon Vineyard
in Santa Cruz produces a wine called 'Old
Telegram' made from Mourvèdre grapes, and a
wine called 'Le Cigare Volant,' which is a blend of
Mourvèdre, Grenache, and Syrah. Both are highly
recommended. Cline Cellars in Contra Costa
County produces an excellent Mourvèdre. *Look
for the '88 and '89 vintages.*)**

California Dry Chenin Blanc Producers

Girard Winery *Napa Valley*
Folie-à-Deux *Napa Valley*†
Seghesio *Russian River Valley*
Guenoc Winery *Lake County*
Villa Mt. Eden Winery *Napa Valley*
Price Range $7–10
Preferred Vintages '89, '90

Easy-to-Find or Alternative Selection

Kenwood Vineyards Zinfandel *Sonoma
County*
Price Range $9–12
Preferred Vintages '87, '88

PAELLA

Each town in Spain seems to have its own version of paella, but saffron and chorizo appear to be the common ingredients. Many use shellfish as a main ingredient. With these preparations try a Spanish white wine from the Penedés or Rioja. For paella whose main ingredients are chicken and sausage, try a Spanish Rioja or Ribera del Duero red.

Spanish White Wine Producers

Torres *Penedés*
Look for Gran Viña Sol
Montecillo *Rioja*
Marqués de Cáceres *Rioja*
Labastida *Rioja*
Martinsancho Verdejo *Rueda*†
Price Range $7–15
Preferred Vintages '88, '89, '90

Spanish Red Rioja Producers

Berberana
Bodegas Olarra
La Rioja Alta
Marqués de Riscal
Bodegas Bretón 'Loriñón'†
Price Range $8–15
Preferred Vintages '85, '87, '88 ('89 to cellar)

Spanish Ribera del Duero Producers

Tinto Pesquera†
Balbás†
Viña Pedrosa†
Price Range $7–18
Preferred Vintages '85, '<u>86</u>, '88 ('89 to cellar)
(Additionally, the producer Bodegas Inviosa
makes a wine called 'Lar de Barros' from the
Estremadura region of Spain that is an excellent
red worth seeking out. *Look for the '86 and '87*
vintages.)

Easy-to-Find or Alternative Selection

Marqués de Cáceres *Rioja*
Price Range $8–15
Preferred Vintages '89, '90

RISOTTO

There are hundreds of preparations for
risotto but all are rich with stock. I
recommend a bottle of good Italian
Pinot Grigio or Pinot Bianco from
northern Italy with most preparations,
but a softer Italian red such as Chianti
Classico is also very flavorful.

Italian Pinot Grigio Producers

Josef Brigl
Gianni Vescovo
Gradnik†
Jermann†
Livio Felluga
Price Range $10–17
Preferred Vintages '89, '90

Italian Pinot Bianco Producers

Enofriulia
Gianni Vescovo
Plozner
Morasutti
Tiefenbrunner
Herrnhofer†
Price Range $7–15
Preferred Vintages '89, '90

Italian Chianti Classico Producers

Aziano
Badia a Coltibuono
Brolio-Ricasoli
Castelgreve
Isole e Olena
Castello di Fonterutoli
Castello di Cacchiano†
Look for Riserva
Tizzano
Price Range $8–15
Preferred Vintages '87, '88, '89

Easy-to-Find or Alternative Selections

Santa Margherita Pinot Grigio
Price Range $14–17
Preferred Vintages '89, '90

Frescobaldi Chianti Classico
Price Range $5–8
Preferred Vintages '89, '90

SALADS

Salads are difficult to match with wines because many have a vinaigrette-based dressing. The vinegar conflicts with the taste of wine and the oil coats the palate. In general, a wine with firm acidity will be the best choice.

CAESAR SALAD

The classic Caesar salad combines the flavors of anchovies, egg yolk, lemon juice, Worcestershire sauce, Parmesan cheese, fresh pepper, olive oil, and fresh croutons with fresh romaine lettuce. This may be the world's favorite salad, and a bottle of French Chablis is the perfect match. A crisp Italian Verdicchio or Soave Classico would be a very nice alternative.

French Chablis Producers

Louis Michel
René & Vincent Dauvissat
Long-Depaquit†
Price Range $15–25
Preferred Vintages '88, '89

Italian Verdicchio Producers

Colonnara 'Cuprese'
Garafoli†
Look for Macrina

Fazi-Battaglia
Umani Ronchi
Look for Casal di Sera
Price Range $7–14
Preferred Vintages (*youngest available*)

Italian Soave Classico Producers

Masi
Look for Col Baraca
Anselmi
Boscaini
Pieropan
Santa Sofia
Price Range $7–12
Preferred Vintages '89, '90

Easy-to-Find or Alternative Selections

Joseph Drouhin Chablis
Price Range $14–18
Preferred Vintages '89, '90

Masi Soave Classico
Price Range $7–10
Preferred Vintages '89, '90

CHICKEN SALAD

Chicken salad can be prepared in a variety of ways. For those done with celery, almonds, and scallions, try a California Sauvignon Blanc or a young French Beaujolais-Villages. For preparations that include raisins, apples, grapes, and nuts, or for oriental preparations using sesame, water chestnuts, and bean sprouts, dry Chenin Blanc from California or Washington, or French Vouvray is pleasant.

California Sauvignon Blanc Producers

Kenwood Vineyards *Sonoma County*
Babcock Vineyards *Santa Ynez Valley*
Beaulieu Vineyards *Napa Valley*
Ferrari-Carano *Sonoma County*
Price Range $7–12
Preferred Vintages '89, '90

French Beaujolais-Villages Producers

Louis Jadot
Joseph Drouhin
Louis Latour
Price Range $10–15
Preferred Vintages '88, '89, '90

California Dry Chenin Blanc Producers

Folie-à-Deux *Napa Valley*†
Girard Winery *Napa Valley*
Pine Ridge Winery *Napa Valley*
Seghesio *Russian River Valley*
Price Range $7–10
Preferred Vintages '89, '90

Washington Dry Chenin Blanc Producers

Covey Run *Yakima Valley*
Hogue Cellars *Washington State*
Chateau Ste. Michelle *Columbia Valley*
Snoqualmie Winery *Washington*
Price Range $5–8
Preferred Vintages '89, '90

French Vouvray Producers

Marc Brédif
Monmousseau
Château Moncontour
Price Range $8–15
Preferred Vintages '89, '90

Easy-to-Find or Alternative Selections

Chateau Ste. Michelle Dry Riesling *Columbia Valley*
Price Range $4–7
Preferred Vintages '89, '90

Georges Duboeuf Beaujolais-Villages
Price Range $7–10
Preferred Vintages '89, '90

SALADE NIÇOISE

Anchovies, tomatoes, Niçoise olives, potatoes, green beans, and often tuna fish combine with lettuce to give salade Niçoise a slightly salty flavor with plenty of character. Try a French Corbières Blanc or Cassis Blanc. Also, a French Côtes-du-Rhône Blanc goes nicely with salade Niçoise.

French Corbières Blanc and Cassis Blanc Producers

Mont Tauch†
Rogue Sestière†
Domaine de Fontsainte 'Gris de Gris'†
Clos Ste. Magdelaine Cassis Blanc†
Price Range $7–14
Preferred Vintages '88, '89

French Côtes-du-Rhône Blanc Producers

E. Guigal
Château du Trignon†
Auguste Clape†
Price Range $8–15
Preferred Vintages '89, '90

La Vieille Ferme Côtes du Lubéron Blanc
Price Range $5–8
Preferred Vintages '88, '89 '90

SEAFOOD LOUIS

Crab, shrimp, egg, and tomatoes are
typically served with Thousand Island or
Russian dressing. This tangy, sweet
flavor is matched nicely by off-dry
whites such as Washington dry white
Riesling or French Vouvray.

**Washington Dry White Riesling
Producers**

Barnard-Griffin *Columbia Valley*†
Hogue Cellars *Washington State*
Louis Facelli *Washington*†
Price Range $6–9
Preferred Vintages '89, '90

French Vouvray Producers

Marc Brédif
Monmousseau
Château Moncontour
Price Range $8–15
Preferred Vintages '89, '90

Easy-to-Find or Alternative Selections

Chateau Ste. Michelle Dry Riesling *Columbia
Valley*
Price Range $4–7
Preferred Vintages '89, '90

SPINACH SALAD

Wonderfully light and often filled with chopped egg, crisp bacon, and cheese, a spinach salad is great with many different dry white wines. Try an Italian Orvieto Classico or a Vernaccia di San Gimignano.

Italian Orvieto Classico Producers

Barbi
Barberani
Bigi†
Look for Vigneto Torricella
Decugnano dei Barbi†
Antinori
Price Range $7–14
Preferred Vintages '89, '90

Italian Vernaccia Producers

Teruzzi & Puthod
Look for Terre di Tufo†
Falchini
San Quirico
Giannina
Price Range $7–18
Preferred Vintages '89, '90

Easy-to-Find or Alternative Selection

Ruffino Orvieto Classico
Price Range $7–10
Preferred Vintages '89, '90

ETHNIC DISHES

Recommending wines to match the vast number of preparations for the different ethnic cuisines is beyond the range of this book. However, there are a few suggestions that are helpful as general guidelines.

CHINESE

Gewürztraminer matches the flavors of red pepper, green onion, water chestnuts, and peanut sauce. Crab, scallops, and black bean sauce are complemented by dry white Riesling or good Vouvray. With spicy chicken, garlic, broccoli, almonds, and duck, try Pinot Noir. Beef, spinach, curry, and five star preparations call for red wines from the Rhône Valley.

JAPANESE

For the more delicate sushis such as tuna (maguro), yellowtail (hamachi), sweet shrimp (ama ebi), and flounder (shiromaki), dry white Bordeaux and Washington Sauvignon Blanc are nice accompaniments. California sparkling wine is another alternative. The more in-

tensely flavored sushis such as squid (ika), salmon (sake), scallops (kaibashira), and octopus (tako), call for a wine with a touch of sweetness, such as an American dry Chenin Blanc or dry white Riesling. For chicken teriyaki and tempura, dry rosé and softer California Pinot Noir offer pleasurable flavor combinations. A medium-bodied red such as California Zinfandel or French Côtes du Roussillon goes nicely with sukiyaki. There are many excellent brands of sake that when served unheated go well with most of the flavors of Japanese cuisine.

THAI

Thai food is a study in contrasts. The varied flavors range from cilantro to coconut milk, peanut sauce to plum. Rice, the mainstay of the cuisine, is accented with contrasting ingredients and frequently prepared with plenty of spice. For the moderately spiced dishes, off-dry whites with firm acidity such as Vouvray, American dry Chenin Blanc, and dry white Riesling are nice complements. For chicken or duck with plum sauce, soft tannin reds such as French Bourgogne Rouge or Oregon and California Pinot Noir are good companions. If the level of spice is intense, one may be better off with a good pilsner or ale.

MEXICAN AND SOUTHWESTERN

Red and green chiles, jalepeño peppers, refried beans, and spicy shredded beef and pork are all intensely flavored and require big, hearty wines. California Zinfandel, Petite Sirah or Syrah, or Rhône Valley reds all stand up to the texture and intensity of many Mexican meals. White wines with plenty of glycerine refresh the palate when served with chicken enchiladas and tamales. Try a California Chardonnay with plenty of body or an American dry Chenin Blanc.

GREEK

Greek cuisine is filled with the flavors of eggplant, garlic, lemon, pine nuts, feta cheese, tomatoes, and rosemary. Fully dry whites such as French white Bordeaux and California Sauvignon Blanc are well matched to many of these flavors. For lamb marinated with rosemary and garlic, try French reds such as Côtes-du-Rhône or Côtes du Roussillon and Italian reds such as Vino Nobile di Montepulciano or Barbera d'Alba. There are also many excellent Greek wines that are unique and fun to have with Greek cuisine. Retsina, a wine that has pine resin added during fermentation, has a powerful flavor that stands up to many oily dishes prepared in the traditional peasant style.

INDIAN

Indian cuisine ranges from mild to fiery. Many dishes are vegetarian, based on either wheat or rice, and, when moderately spiced, these are nicely complemented by the taste of young American Riesling and Gewürztraminer. French Beaujolais-Villages is an alternative if red wine is preferred. If the level of spice is intense, one might be better off with a good pilsner or ale.

MIDDLE EASTERN

I like softer reds with Middle Eastern food. French Beaujolais-Villages and Italian Chianti Classico are flavorful complements to tahini (sesame paste), roasted eggplant, and lamb. Hummos and Baba Ghannouj can be matched with crisp Italian whites such as Vernaccia di San Gimignano and Pinot Grigio.

DESSERTS

While some desserts are well complemented by wine, many should be served first and the wine afterward. The sweetness of most pies, the texture of many cakes, and the coldness of ice cream and sorbet make these desserts to be served alone. For other desserts, look to the dominant flavor to find an appropriate wine. It is often difficult to find dessert wines other than ports and sherries outside of specialty wine stores, so in this section I have omitted the easy-to-find or alternative recommendation.

FLAVORS

CHOCOLATE

Can any wine match the complex flavor of Belgian chocolate? Yes! Banyuls, the vins doux naturels from the Côtes du Roussillon district of France have a unique quality that make them the perfect wines to serve with chocolate. They are well worth seeking out! American Black Muscat has the aroma of roses and also goes nicely with chocolate. Late bottled Vintage Port and

aged Tawny Port also complement chocolate desserts. An unusual but exceptionally nice combination with chocolate is French rosé Champagne.

French Banyuls Producers

Domaine du Mas Blanc (Dr. Parcé)†
Domaine de Paulilles (Robert Doutres)†
Price Range $10–25
Preferred Vintages '85, '86, '88

American Black Muscat Producers

Andrew Quady 'Elysium' *California*
Thurston Wolfe *Washington*†
Price Range $6–9 (in 375 ml bottles)
(Note: Black Muscat is not an actual variety but a name associated with dark-skinned Muscat grapes.)

Late Bottled Vintage Port Producers

Taylor Fladgate Late Bottled Vintage Port
Fonseca Late Bottled Port
Warre's Late Bottled Vintage Port
Price Range $10–30

Well-Aged Tawny Port Producers

Graham's Twenty-Year-Old Tawny
Dow's 'Boardroom'
Warre's 'Grand Reserve'
Price Range $20–40
(Additionally, Bonny Doon Vineyard in California's Santa Cruz Mountains produces an infusion of Raspberry essence called 'Framboise', that is a wonderful wine to have with desserts combining the flavors or chocolate and raspberries.)

French Rosé Champagne Producers

Pol Roger & Cie. *Épernay*
A. Charbaut & Fils *Épernay*
Louis Roederer *Reims*
Philipponnat *Mareuil-sur-Aÿ*
Veuve Clicquot-Ponsardin Brut *Reims*
Price Range $30–50

APPLE

The taste of apple in a tart or with cinnamon in apple crisp is nicely matched by German Riesling of Auslese quality or French Muscat Beaumes-de-Venise. Late harvest Riesling from either Washington or California is a pleasant alternative.

German Riesling Auslese Producers

Egon Müller Scharzhöfberger *Saar*†
Milz Trittenheimer Felsenkopf *Mosel*†
Schloss Saarstein Serriger Schloss Saarsteiner *Saar*†
Look for Gold Capsule
Schloss Groenesteyn Rüdesheimer Berg Schlossberg *Rheingau*†
Fritz Haag Brauneberger Juffer Sonnenuhr *Mosel*†
J. J. Prüm Wehlener Sonnenuhr *Mosel*†
Mönchhof Ürziger Würzgarten *Mosel*†
Dr. Loosen Erdener Prälat *Mosel*†
Price Range $18–30
Preferred Vintages '83, '85, '88, '89

French Muscat Beaumes-de-Venise Producers

Domaine Durban
Paul Jaboulet-Aîné

Domaine St.-Sauveur
Domaine de Coyeux†
Price Range $8–12 (in 375 ml bottles)
Preferred Vintages '88, '89 '90

American Late-Harvest Riesling Producers

Hogue Cellars *Washington State*
Kiona Vineyards *Columbia Valley*†
Stewart Vineyards *Yakima Valley*†
Babcock Vineyards Santa *Ynez Valley*
Hidden Cellars *Mendocino*†
Chateau Ste. Jean *Sonoma Valley*
Joseph Phelps Vineyards *Napa Valley*
Look for Special Select
Price Range $8–15 (in 375 ml bottles)
Preferred Vintages '87, '89

PEAR

The sweet spice of late-harvest Gewürz-traminer marries well with the flavor of pear. Additionally, German Riesling of Spätlese quality with some bottle age can be excellent. *Care must be taken to assure that older Spätlese have been stored properly.*

American Late-Harvest Gewürztraminer Producers

Arbor Crest *Columbia Valley*†
Kiona Vineyards *Columbia Valley*†
Mark West Vineyards *Sonoma*†
Chateau St. Jean *Sonoma*†
Navarro *Sonoma Valley*†
De Loach Vineyards *Sonoma County*†
Price Range $10–30
Preferred Vintages '87, '89

German Riesling Spätlese Producers

Schloss Saarstein Serriger Schloss Saarsteiner *Saar*†

Selbach-Oster Graacher Himmelreich *Mosel*†

Domdechant Werner Hochheimer Domdechaney *Rheingau*†

Langwerth Von Simmern Rauenthaler Baiken *Rheingau*†

Fritz Haag Brauneberger Juffer Sonnenuhr *Mosel*†

Dr. Loosen Erdener Prälat *Mosel*†

Price Range $18–30

Preferred Vintages '83, '85, '88

STRAWBERRY AND CHERRY

Strawberry and cherry flavors are both nicely enhanced by American Black Muscat and French Sauternes.

American Black Muscat Producers

Andrew Quady 'Elysium' *California*

Thurston Wolfe *Washington*†

Price Range $6–9 (in 375 ml bottles)

(Note: Black Muscat is not an actual variety but a name associated with dark-skinned Muscat grapes.)

French Sauternes Producers

Château Rieussec *Sauternes*

Château Filhot *Sauternes*

Château Nairac *Sauternes*†

Château Coutet *Barsac*

Château Les Justices *Sauternes*

Château de Malle *Sauternes*

Price Range $14–30 (in 375 ml bottles)

Preferred Vintages '83, '86, '88 ('89 to cellar)

RASPBERRY AND BLACKBERRY

German Rieslings of Auslese quality are excellent with raspberry and blackberry flavors, as is an American Black Muscat.

German Riesling Auslese Producers

Milz Trittenheimer Felsenkopf *Mosel*†
Schloss Groenesteyn Rüdesheimer Berg Schlossberg *Rheingau*†
Fritz Haag Brauneberger Juffer-Sonnenuhr *Mosel*†
J. J. Prüm Wehlener Sonnenuhr *Mosel*†
Langwerth Von Simmern Hattenheimer Nussbrunnen *Rheingau*†
Dr. Loosen Erdener Prälat *Mosel*†
Price Range $18–30
Preferred Vintages '83, '85, '88, '89

American Black Muscat Producers

Andrew Quady 'Elysium' *California*
Thurston Wolfe *Washington*†
Price Range $6–9 (in 375 ml bottles)
(Note: Black Muscat is not an actual variety but a name associated with dark-skinned Muscat grapes.)

PEACH AND APRICOT

The flavors of peach and apricot are well suited to German Rieslings of Auslese quality and to California Orange Muscat. French Sauternes is another fine complement.

German Riesling Auslese Producers

Egon Müller Scharzhofberger *Saar*†
Milz Trittenheimer Felsenkopf *Mosel*†

Schloss Groenesteyn Rüdesheimer Berg Schlossberg *Rheingau*†
Fritz Haag Brauneberger Juffer-Sonnenuhr *Mosel*†
J. J. Prüm Wehlener Sonnenuhr *Mosel*†
Mönchhof Ürziger Würzgarten *Mosel*†
Dr. Loosen Erdener Prälat *Mosel*†
Price Range $18–40
Preferred Vintages '83, '85, '88, '89

California Orange Muscat Producers

Andrew Quady 'Essencia' *California*
Santino *Amador County*
Price Range $6–9 (in 375 ml bottles)

French Sauternes Producers

Château Rieussec *Sauternes*
Château Filhot *Sauternes*
Château Doisy-Védrines *Barsac*
Château Rabaud-Promis *Sauternes*†
Château Les Justices *Sauternes*
Château de Malle *Sauternes*
Price Range $14–30 (in 375 ml bottles)
Preferred Vintages '83, '86, '88 ('89 to cellar)
(The Loire Valley in France yields many excellent dessert wines from late-harvested Chenin Blanc grapes. Often hard to find but well worth seeking out are Domaine des Baumard 'Quarts de Chaume' and 'Coteaux du Layon.' *Look for the '89 vintage*.)

LEMON

For desserts that have lemon as the dominant flavor, California dessert-style Muscat Blanc and California Orange Muscat are preferred.

California Dessert-style Muscat Blanc Producers

Beaulieu Vineyards 'Muscat de Frontignan' *California*

Robert Mondavi Winery 'Moscato d'Oro' *Napa Valley*

Robert Pecota 'Muscato di Andrea' *Napa Valley*

Louis Martini 'Moscato Amabile' *Napa Valley*†
Price Range $8–12

(Additionally, Bonny Doon Vineyard makes an excellent dessert wine called 'Vin de Glacière' from Muscat Blanc [Canelli] grapes that have been frozen prior to vinification. *Look for the '89 vintage.*)

California Orange Muscat Producers

Andrew Quady 'Essencia' *California*
Santino *Amador County*
Price Range $6–9 (in 375 ml bottles)

ALMOND AND HAZELNUT

Malmsey from Madeira and French Sauternes are both excellent matches with the flavors of almond or hazelnut. For nut tarts rich with the meat of a variety of nuts, try a California botrytised Sauvignon Blanc/Semillon.

Madeira Malmsey Producers

Blandy's
Look for 10 Year Old
Cossart Gordon

Shortridge & Lawton
D'Oliveiras
Price Range $12–25
(Madeira is one of the longest lived of all wines. True vintage bottlings of Madeira dating back to the early 1900s are still available, albeit expensive.)

French Sauternes Producers

Château Rieussec *Sauternes*
Château Filhot *Sauternes*
Château Doisy-Védrines *Barsac*
Château Rabaud-Promis *Sauternes*†
Château Les Justices *Sauternes*
Château de Malle *Sauternes*
Price Range $14–30 (in 375 ml bottles)
Preferred Vintages '83, '86, '88, ('89 to cellar)

California Botrytised Sauvignon Blanc/Semillon Producers

Robert Mondavi Winery *Napa Valley*
Monticello Cellars 'Chateau M' *Napa Valley*
Joseph Phelps Vineyards 'Délices de Semillon'
  Napa Valley
Price Range $8–15+ (in 375 ml bottles)
Preferred Vintages '87, '89
(The firm of Peter Lehmann in Australia produces a superb botrytised Semillon Sauternes from grapes of the Barossa Valley. *Look for the '88 and '89 vintages.*)

WALNUT

Walnuts and Tawny Port are a classic combination. The aroma of Tawny Port is similar to that of walnuts.

Tawny Port Producers

Graham's
Fonseca

Dow's
Warre's
Taylor Fladgate
Smith-Woodhouse
Croft
Quinta do Noval
Price Range $8–15 +
**(Ficklin Vineyards and Andrew Quady from
California both produce very good port wines
that are worth seeking out. In Washington,
Whidbey's produces a vintage port. *Look for the
'87 vintage.*)**

STILTON CHEESE

Stilton is a perfect cheese to serve with
late bottled Vintage Ports, single
vineyard Vintage Ports and well-aged
Tawny Ports.

Late Bottled Vintage Port Producers

Taylor Fladgate Late Bottled Vintage Port
Fonseca Late Bottled Port
Warre's Late Bottled Vintage Port
Price Range $10–30

Single Vineyard Vintage Port Producers

Graham's 'Quinta Dos Malvados' Vintage Port
Dow's 'Quinta Do Bomfim' Vintage Port
Price Range $18–30

Well-Aged Tawny Port Producers

Graham's Twenty-Year-Old Tawny
Dow's 'Boardroom'
Warre's 'Grand Reserve'
Price Range $20–40

Easy-to-Find or Alternative Selection
Sandeman's Founder's Reserve Port
Price Range $10–15

CHEESECAKE

California Orange Muscat and French Muscat Beaumes-de-Venise match the texture and flavor of many different cheesecakes, particularly those that aren't topped with fruit. Sauternes goes very nicely with cheesecake that has a fruit topping.

California Orange Muscat Producers

Andrew Quady 'Essencia' *California*
Santino *Amador County*
Price Range $6–9 (in 375 ml bottles)
(Additionally, Bonny Doon Vineyard makes an excellent dessert wine called 'Vin de Glacière' from Muscat Blanc [Canelli] grapes that have been frozen prior to vinification. *Look for the '89 vintage.)*

French Muscat Beaumes-de-Venise Producers

Domaine Durban
Paul Jaboulet-Aîné
Domaine St.-Sauveur
Domaine de Coyeux†
Price Range $8–12 (in 375 ml bottles)
Preferred Vintages '88, '89, '90

French Sauternes Producers

Château Rieussec *Sauternes*
Château Filhot *Sauternes*

Château Nairac *Sauternes*†
Château Rabaud-Promis *Sauternes*†
Château Les Justices *Sauternes*
Château Coutet *Barsac*
Price Range $14–30 (in 375 ml bottles)
Preferred Vintages '83, '86, '88, ('89 to cellar)

CRÈME CARAMEL

Both French Muscat Beaumes-de-
Venise and Malmsey from Madeira are
marvelous complements with the rich
taste of crème caramel.

French Muscat Beaumes-de-Venise Producers

Domaine Durban
Paul Jaboulet-Aîné
Domaine St.-Sauveur
Domaine de Coyeux†
Price Range $8–12 (in 375 ml bottles)
Preferred Vintages '88, '89, '90

Madeira Malmsey Producers

Blandy's
Look for 10 Year Old
Cossart Gordon
Shortridge & Lawton
D'Oliveiras
Price Range $12–25
**(A rare and wonderful Malmsey-style wine called
Malvasia de Sitges is made by the Cellars J.
Robert in the Cataluña region of Spain. It
perfectly complements Crème Caramel.)**

TIRAMISÙ

This popular espresso-laced Italian dessert is light and delicate but flavorful enough to stand up to Italian Vin Santo and California dessert-style Muscat Blanc.

Italian Vin Santo Producers

Isole e Olena†
Avignonesi†
Lungarotti
Antinori
Capezzana
Price Range $14–25 (in 375 ml bottles)

California Dessert-style Muscat Blanc Producers

Beaulieu Vineyards 'Muscat de Frontignan' *California*
Robert Mondavi Winery 'Moscato d'Oro' *Napa Valley*
Robert Pecota 'Muscato di Andrea' *Napa Valley*
Louis Martini 'Moscato Amabile' *Napa Valley*†
Price Range $8–12

(Additionally, Bonny Doon Vineyard makes an excellent dessert wine called 'Vin de Glacière' from Muscat Blanc [Canelli] grapes that have been frozen prior to vinification. *Look for the '89 vintage.*)

ZABAGLIONE

Marsala and egg yolks whipped with sugar make up this classic Italian dessert. To match its light and bright flavor, try an Italian Vin Santo or a Malmsey from Madeira. As an alternative, try a French Muscat Beaumes-de-Venise.

Italian Vin Santo Producers

Isole e Olena†
Avignonesi†
Lungarotti
Antinori
Capezzana
Price Range $14–25 (in 375 ml bottles)

Madeira Malmsey Producers

Blandy's
Look for 10-Year-Old
Cossart Gordon
Shortridge & Lawton
D'Oliveiras
Price Range $12–25

French Muscat Beaumes-de-Venise Producers

Domaine Durban
Paul Jaboulet-Aîné
Domaine St.-Sauveur
Domaine de Coyeux†
Price Range $8–12 (in 375 ml bottles)
Preferred Vintages '88, '89, '90

BUYING AND STORING WINE, AND PARTY PLANNING

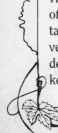

VINTAGES

A vintage is merely a year, but a "vintage year" is special. It happens when the weather throughout the entire growing season for the vine has the total result of yielding excellent grapes. Great wines, however, are made in the cellars after the harvest is complete. It is the combination of the climate of the region during the year and the talent of the winemaker that makes great wine possible. John Melville in his *Guide to California Wines* published in 1955 recognized that "the ultimate guarantee of quality for a table or any other wine is the reputation of the winegrower or producer." In this book I have listed, where appropriate, preferred vintages that will be available at the time of publication. There are many older vintages that may be available and that are very good wines, but this will be dependent upon the supply in your local market. I hope that the preferred vintage recommendations will offer suggestions without creating expectations. Many producers are able to make high-quality wines in vintages that are not considered "vintage years." Remember, it can be more fun to discover a great wine from an off year than to simply find what you expect.

BUYING OLDER VINTAGES

Many older vintage wines are available for purchase in wine shops or liquor and grocery store wine sections. Care should be taken to examine a wine's condition before purchase. Check the fill level in the bottle to be sure the ullage, or loss through evaporation, has not dropped the level below the bottom of the neck. If possible, examine the color of the wine by looking at it through the neck against a light. Be sure the color is not overly brown. Aged white wines should not have an amber color unless they are sherries or dessert wines. Well-stored red wines may have amber edges but their dominant color should still be red. There are exceptions to these rules, but the risk of purchase is your decision. It is advisable to ask about the storage conditions of an older wine prior to purchase. Why is it available now? Where has this wine been stored? If the merchant can't answer these basic questions, the risk may not be worth taking. Good merchants will have asked these same questions of their suppliers and will know the wine's storage history. Sadly, the storage conditions of many importers' and wholesalers' warehouses are not adequate to age wine properly. Older stocks may have been subjected to extremes of temperature or humidity, and the wines may have been damaged.

CELLARING WINE

There are various reasons for starting a wine cellar. Many people cellar wine in order to have a pantry to go to when they are looking for a dinner wine. Others wish to keep a supply of mature wines available on an ongoing basis. Some are desirous of cellaring wine to benefit from its appreciation in value.

Storage conditions range from dark corners of basements to temperature-controlled cellars with state-of-the-art storage conditions. The proper temperature for storing wine has been written about to the point where consumers have an exaggerated concern about their cellar temperature and not enough concern about light, vibration, and humidity. Ultraviolet light and vibration are both deadly to wine. It is important that the storage area be out of direct light sources and free of vibration through walls and storage racks. Avoid locating wine racks near appliances such as furnaces, washer/driers, and under stairwells. The wine should be stored within a temperature range of 40–65 degrees F. Gradual temperature changes are not harmful to wines that are cellared for short-term aging.

If a large cellar of fine wine is held for long-term aging, a temperature-controlled environment is advisable, and it is mandatory if the wine is being held for investment. Humidity is a major consideration for a wine cellar. Cellars that are too dry do not keep corks moist enough to prevent ullage, the gradual lowering of the fill level inside the bottle. If you have stored wine for less than two years and you notice the fill levels dropping, you should consider installing a temperature/humidty control unit. Many companies make wine storage units. The price of the wines being cellared should also be considered. If you are aging medium-priced to expensive wines, it is probably worth considering the purchase of a temperature/humidty control unit. Better storage conditions help improve the chances that your wine will be at its best when you serve it.

AGING WINE

How long to age wine is subjective, and there are many different ideas on this subject. I believe that each wine must be considered individually in order to determine how long it should be cellared. One thing is certain though, your wine is changing in the cellar. When you decide to age wine, you are undertaking a task that requires maintenance. It is all too easy to purchase wine, put it in the cellar, and forget about it. The result can be disappointing. Older wine books referred to the aging potential of the wines that were made when these books were written. Today, wines are being made for earlier consumption and many may not last as long as these older references imply. Regular checks of the inventory in your cellar should be made to determine which wines need to be consumed. It is recommended that you keep a cellar list and use it for planning. For insurance reasons, it is also helpful to keep a periodically updated cellar list outside the home. Check with your insurance agent to be sure that your cellar is properly insured.

As wines age, the freshness and fruitiness change as the tannins soften. Care should be taken to assure that the wine is consumed before the fruit fades. Many leathery, old reds can be remarkable, but many others aren't so sound. Consult with a wine merchant about which wines to cellar for long periods of time. Many people age wines long past their prime merely because it is widely assumed that the older, the better. This simply isn't true.

PARTY PLANNING

What to Consider

There are many things to consider when deciding how much wine to have on hand for a party. The number of guests is just the beginning. Folks of different age groups consume different amounts of different beverages. If there is an open bar where liquor will be served, less wine is likely to be consumed. If beer is available, a number of guests will opt for beer rather than wine. The duration of the event is one of the most important considerations. Over the years, I have developed a simple formula that has worked for hundreds of weddings, parties, and get togethers.

Number of Guests

The number of guests can vary from 6 to 600, but this is the major variable.

Duration of the Event

The amount of wine guests will consume will vary, to a point, with the number of hours the event will last. If the party is for a group of 25 or more, figure the following:

1–2 hours	6 ounces per person
2–3 hours	8 ounces per person
3–4 hours	10 ounces per person
A dinner	12 ounces per person

For dinner parties of 6 to 8 people, the simple rule is to have one bottle of wine with each course being served, except for the main course, where multiple bottles may be desired. Additionally, it may be desirable to have extra aperitif wine as all guests may not arrive at the same time.

The Formula

1. Determine the number of hours.
   (e.g., 3 hours or 8 ounces per person)
2. Determine the number of people.
   (e.g., 50 people)
3. Multiply the number of ounces times the number of people.
   (e.g., 8 oz × 50 people = 400 ounces)
4. Divide the total ounces by 25.4 ounces (per 750 ml bottle)
   (e.g., 400 ÷ 25.4 = 15.7 or 16 bottles)

The quantity needed for a group of 50 for a three-hour party is one case plus 4 bottles of wine, which, if rounded up, is a case and a half of wine. This allows a small surplus for the house, well deserved for all the effort.

ABOUT THE AUTHOR

Daniel McCarthy is co-founder and co-owner of McCarthy & Schiering Wine Merchants in Seattle, Washington. He has appeared on local radio and television, speaks regularly at wine auctions, and judges wine competitions across the country, including the Atlanta International Wine Fair, the Western Washington State Fair, and the Auction of Northwest Wines. He and his wife are the proud owners of two English cocker spaniels.